Free To Lead:

10 Women of the Bible God Empowered to Lead

How to Maximize Your God-given Potential

With gratitude —

Rita Carver

RITA WHITE CARVER, PhD

xulon PRESS

Dedicated to my sister, Marti,
God's gift to us all.

CONTENTS

INTRODUCTION

✣

For my daughter Heather,
May you always have the freedom to choose.

*T*penned those words in the mid-1980s in the front of a book
about women in the workplace. I considered myself some-
what of a pioneer blazing a path so the next generation of women—
including my daughter—would have choices. I wished for them the
freedom to be whoever they wanted to be: single or married; with
children or without; a stay-at-home mom or a mom who loved both
her children and her career.

Back then, whatever I chose seemed wrong. When I went to work,
my female friends, including my mother, thought I was depriving my
children. "You will ruin your children," I was told. With my career, I
was always juggling work assignments with days when the kids were
sick or simply out of school. I didn't feel I could devote myself to
give 100% to anything. Using my Rita-math, I figured I was giving
motherhood about 80% and my career about 80%. When I added
the two numbers together, I came up with 160%. Wasn't that more
than enough?

I was also fighting as a woman to enjoy the freedom to lead and
be who God created me to be. I grew up in an evangelical home and

religious tradition where women did not lead, and they did not speak. According to the script I was given, my role, as a woman, was to be a wife and mother. I was to be silent, submissive and to serve. These expressions of Christian discipleship were not in my experience the beautiful demonstration of a loving, caring congregation, but rather characteristics that made me as a woman feel like a second-class citizen in the family of God especially when serving always involved the nursery or kitchen. When I had a spiritual or biblical question, I was supposed to ask my husband or maybe the pastor. God spoke to men, not women.

When I began my married life in Wisconsin, a minister again reminded me that God did not create women to speak or to lead. My conclusion was that as a woman I did not matter to God—that God could not use my brains or my voice. So why did an all-knowing, infinite God waste brains on women if we were simply to be silent?

Decades later, I was still asking the question. I had enjoyed success in business working as a consultant with nonprofit organizations where I learned to lead from what Ronald Heifetz called the foot of the table—"the domain to which women have been restricted for ages."[1] As I began my doctoral program to earn my PhD in leadership studies from Dallas Baptist University, I was eager to research the women of the Bible. I wanted to see if there were any women leaders, and if so, I wanted to understand how they led.

God's Message for Women—and Men

What I discovered in scripture shattered my perspective on how God views women and what He expects of us as His daughters. I found a God who celebrates His children as leaders—both male and female. As I examined the biblical accounts of women through the lens of leadership, my religious traditions were challenged. God spoke to women. God empowered women. He entrusted women with His message to deliver to His people. He allowed them the freedom to lead. Does that mean that we as Christian women today are free to lead? As you journey through this study with me, we will answer that question together.

In this book, you and I will meet Esther, a young woman who did what she was told until tragedy struck; Rahab, a woman who was willing to take risks; and Deborah, a woman in authority who stood by a man at his moment of weakness. We will look at the crucial tasks given to Martha, the woman of Samaria, and Mary Magdalene to deliver God's message of truth. We will celebrate the courage of Mary of Bethany and the wise woman of Abel who stood up in the face of challenge. We will be inspired by the actions of a mother and a businesswoman. These biblical women are examples of what God wants to do through your life and mine. God has spoken and continues to speak to women. He then invites them to share His message with others. Like the women of the Bible, God wants to use you and me. He has granted us the freedom to lead.

The Challenge

As I have shared this message with friends and family, I am aware that the premise of this book is contrary to what many of us grew up believing as truth from our various church backgrounds. Some of the biblical accounts, especially of Martha and the woman of Samaria, were so contrary to what I was taught that I felt like someone pressed the red "panic" button on my internal key fob. The lights blinked. The horn blared, and my mind said: Jesus did what? He entrusted this basic biblical truth to a woman. Really?

3

One of my early conversations about my book was with my father-in-law, Paul, a godly man, who simply shook his head after reading my manuscript and said, "I have been taught my whole life that women should not lead. Now you are showing me God used women to lead."

The purpose of this book is not to challenge what you or I believe about God. It is not to diminish our belief in the Bible as ultimate truth. It is to raise the possibility that truth has been distorted through our cultural traditions. The message of this book is that God created both women and men with the freedom to lead. Your opportunity and responsibility is to examine scripture for yourself and answer the question: What does the Bible teach about women and leadership?[2]

What Is Leadership?

Leadership is sometimes misunderstood as being the private world of a few specially gifted, charismatic individuals. Some believe leadership to be the sacred ground for professionals and graduate students. Actually, according to James Kouzes and Barry Posner, two scholars who have studied leadership for over 25 years, leadership is a process that allows ordinary people to bring forth the best in themselves in the pursuit of leading others.[3] You lead when you inspire your children. You lead when you guide a group of women in Bible study. You lead when you care for others.

I like Donald T. Phillips's definition of leadership best:

Leadership is leaders acting—as well as caring, inspiring, and persuading others to act—for certain shared goals that represent the values—the wants and needs, the aspirations and expectations—of themselves and the people they represent.[4]

Phillips defines what leadership is, but what I searched for was the "how" to lead. How can I as a woman become a leader who honors God?

The leadership model I selected is built on the life and leadership of Christian business pioneer, Mary C. Crowley, as well as the ten women from scripture. (For more information about Mary Crowley and her leadership, please see the insert at the end of the introduction.) The model is built on three major leadership concepts: authentic leadership, strengths-based leadership, and servant leadership.

Authentic Leadership: Who Are You Authentically?

The concept embraces the fact that to lead, you begin with who you are—the person God created you to be. Too often we are tempted to try and copy another's leadership style. Leadership always requires us to be our authentic selves—not copies of someone else. We will examine this aspect of leadership further in the lives of women like Esther and Deborah.

Strengths-based Leadership: What Are Your God-given Gifts?

Leaders utilize their strengths, their gifts. They focus on what they can do—not on what they can't do. Sometimes as women, we confuse our God-given gifts with our skills. We will examine more about this facet of leadership in the life of Mary of Bethany.

Servant Leadership: What Is Your Passion? Whom Do You Have a Heart to Serve?

Leadership involves taking action on behalf of others. As we saw in our definition by Donald Phillips, leadership involves "caring, inspiring, and persuading others to act for certain shared goals."[5] Without action, we are not leaders; we are merely women with good intentions. As unique individuals, God places on each of our hearts certain projects or segments of the population for whom we are passionate. Taking action like Rahab and the woman of Samaria on behalf of those they care about is what allows leaders to make a difference in the world.

"Free-to-Lead" Leadership Model[6]

Each of these components will be analyzed and discussed further as we meet the ten women of the Bible, individual female leaders and ask together: How did they lead? The leadership model we are using can best be illustrated as three concentric circles, which spiral throughout our lives allowing us to continue to grow and develop our leadership.

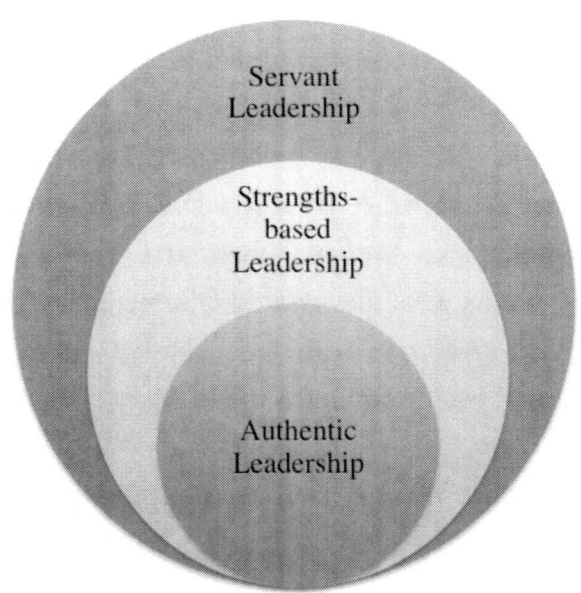

My Personal Journey

The book is also my story—what I have learned through the blessings and brokenness of my life as I searched to know God and understand His desire for women. Author Carol Kuykendall, an expert on storytelling, states, "We are most useful [to God and each other] when we're willing to share our honest stories about the brokenness in our lives." My prayer is that you too will identify God's hand in your life as I share my journey through tragedy and triumph.

Through my experiences and study of scripture, I know for certain God loves us as women. He speaks to us and empowers us to lead. The question I ask myself almost every day is: Am I listening to God speak in the everyday situations of my life? What is He saying to me? How does He want to use me so others can hear His voice of love? What step can I take to begin to make the difference?

Today God is speaking to you. He needs your voice and mine—the voice of His daughters. He wants to empower you and me to communicate His love to others. Are you ready? God wants to use you to make a difference. I hope through the pages of this book, you will sense God's voice as He invites you to be His hands, His message, and His expression of love to a needy world.

MARY C. CROWLEY
1915-1986

Pioneer Christian Business Leader,
Founder of Home Interiors and Gifts, Inc.

*D*uring the 1950s when banks didn't lend money to women and women were often viewed as "little housewives,"[1] Mary Carter Crowley blazed a path through the world of direct sales empowering women to experience personal success and economic liberation. Within twenty-five years of starting her company, Home Interiors & Gifts, Inc., Mary could boast of a salesforce of over 38,000 women and gross annual sales of over $400 million.[2] Her financial success opened the doors for her to lead in business, government and religion.

She was the first woman elected to the board of the Billy Graham Evangelistic Association, the board of the Mercantile Bank of Dallas, and the board of the Direct Sales Association. She was the first female member of the Dallas Chamber of Commerce. She served as a business advisor to President Jimmy Carter, and a friend to President Ronald Reagan and his wife. With her financial resources, she personally saved two colleges and invested in thousands of young people. Throughout her lifetime, she received numerous awards including Southern Methodist University's (SMU) Entrepreneur of the Year and the Horatio Alger Award for Free Enterprise. Dick Bartlett in his book, *The Direct Option*, identifies Mary Crowley and her friend, Mary Kay Ash of Mary Kay, Inc., as the founding mothers of direct sales.[3]

Mary Crowley helped the women who worked with her develop their God-given leadership potential. Her leadership style grew out of her personal life experiences: a childhood tragedy, a failed marriage, the everyday hardship of raising two kids as a single mother, and her run-in with the concrete ceiling of business. Mary was a fighter who did not hear the word "No." Her life motto became: "If it is to be, it is up to me." Crowley's leadership became the focus of my dissertation. Her life, her stories, and her philosophy guided me on my leadership journey to help me define how successful Christian women lead.[4]

CHAPTER ONE

WITHOUT A VOICE: ESTHER
Esther 1:1-10:3

The place you are right now God circled on a map for you.
Ibraham Hafiz

I cannot begin to tell you how ill prepared I was to minister in a farming community. I am a city girl—one of those individuals who on college choir tour is out in the barn taking photos of the cows because they have such lovely brown eyes and are so cute. I was also a new bride, married a total of fourteen days when my husband and I moved to a small town in southern Wisconsin where he was to serve as an assistant pastor. He rented a furnished apartment I did not see until the day we moved in. The "apartment" was the upstairs of an old farmhouse, furnished with two twin beds and a king-size pink bathtub.

Fortunately, the ladies in the congregation were gracious, kind, and patient with me. They taught me to snap beans, can tomatoes and make homemade bread. They brought me candles, placemats, and a television to help turn our small apartment into a home. In short, they loved me so adjusting to country living was not the challenging part of my new life.

The hard part was learning to be the wife of a minister, albeit an assistant pastor. I had ambition, energy, and ideas. I had just graduated from Moody Bible Institute in Chicago. During my last two years at Moody, my husband and I dated. We were best friends and talked about everything. I openly shared my ideas with him.

When we moved to Wisconsin, I got involved in the church and worked in the children's ministry and the music ministry. I continued to express my thoughts with my husband, even in the presence of other church members. During choir practice one evening, where my husband served as the choir director and I as the church pianist, I made a minor suggestion to help the altos find the correct note to sing. That soon landed me in the pastor's office where I was told a woman has her place. She is to learn in silence—in submission to her husband. I listened, but apparently I didn't get it.

Several weeks later, I was back in the pastor's office this time with my husband present. Once again, I had voiced an opinion publicly. During the rehearsal for the children's Christmas program, I had suggested to my husband that perhaps the eight and nine-year-old "shepherds" should enter from a side door rather than from the back of the auditorium in order to save time.

"If you don't learn to be silent," the pastor exhorted me, "you will ruin your husband's ministry."

I went home in tears, brokenhearted. My soul was pierced. Was God, through His servant—Pastor C, really speaking for God? I assumed so. My early childhood teachings reinforced this message. God spoke to men—especially men of God—preachers.

My response was to stop being me. I learned the art of being silent, hiding behind a mask. Recently I came across a poem, which was written more than one hundred years ago, which expressed the feeling of my heart.

We wear the mask that grins and lies,
It hides our cheeks and shades our eyes,—
This debt we pay to human guile;
With torn and bleeding hearts we smile,
And mouth the myriad subtleties.

Why should the world be over-wise,
In counting all our tears and sighs?
Nay, let them only see us, while
We wear the mask.

We smile, but, O great Christ, our cries
To thee from tortured souls arise.
We sing, but oh, the clay is vile
Beneath our feet, and long the mile;
But let the world dream otherwise,
We wear the mask!
—Paul Lawrence Dunbar[1]

Many years later, my experience with Pastor C became one of many reasons I began asking: How should a woman lead? How did God use the women of the Bible to lead His people? Was silence really required? Why was God wasting such potential on women if He expected them to live in silence? Then I discovered the biblical story of Esther. Like me, for many years, this woman simply lived in silence—doing what she was told.

Meeting Esther

The Setting (Esther 1)

The book of Esther opens with a national crisis, which takes place during the reign of the Persian king, Xerxes, who ruled from 486-465 BCE. (His name is translated into Hebrew in the Old Testament as Ahasuerus.) For 180 days the king put on a banquet for his princes and official leaders displaying the splendor of his accomplishments. The celebration ended with a seven-day banquet for the people who lived in the capital city of Susa where the king's palace was located. On the last day of his celebration, the king decided to show off the beauty of his queen to his guests. Scripture reads, *"On the seventh day, when King Xerxes was in high spirits from wine, he commanded the seven eunuchs ... to bring before him Queen Vashti, wearing her royal crown, in order to display her beauty to the people"* (Esther 1:10-11).

Queen Vashti refused to come at the king's command—publicly disobeying the king. Of course as women, we can identify numerous reasons the queen would not want to appear before the king after he and his subjects had been drinking for seven days. We can imagine all types of lewd behavior the king might request of his wife as he showed off her beauty. Would he ask her to disrobe? Perform some type of sexual act in the presence of this multitude? We don't know.

What we do know is that Queen Vashti told the king, "No." She would not come and appear before him, setting in motion an entirely new set of problems.

The wise men quickly pointed out that the queen's disobedience was not only against the king, but against the nobles and all the people throughout the kingdom. As one of the wise men, Memucan, explained, *"For the queen's conduct will become known to all the women, and so they will despise their husbands . . . [and] there will be no end of disrespect and discord"* (1:17-18).

Ultimately, under the king's authority, a decree was written banishing Queen Vashti from ever again appearing before the king. Chapter 1 of Esther ends, *"when the king's edict is proclaimed throughout all his vast realm, all the women will respect their husbands, from the least to the greatest"* (1:20). Another version translates the king's edict as saying: *"husbands should have complete control over their wives and children"* (1:21, CEV). I find it humorous that this book of the Bible, which so clearly celebrates the leadership of a woman, begins with an edict to keep woman in her place.

The Opportunity (Esther 2)

With the banishment of Queen Vashti, the king needed a new woman to become queen. A kingdom-wide search began to bring all the *"beautiful young virgins"* to the harem at the city of Susa (Esther 2:2). One of the girls taken in the roundup was a young woman known as Esther.

Scripture does not reveal a lot about Esther's background. She was a Jew whose Hebrew name was Hadassah. Her great-grandfather was captured in Jerusalem and brought to Babylonia, what is known today as Persia, under Nebuchadnezzar. Some time after Hadassah was born, her parents died. We are not told how they died, or why. Her cousin Mordecai adopted her as his own daughter, and called her by her Persian name, Esther (2: 5-7).

Childhood tragedy marked Esther's growing up years. Now as a teenager, Esther's crises continued. She was rounded up with many other young girls to live at the king's palace and prepare for a one-night tryst with the king. Although we may want to glamorize the spa treatment and special foods, these young women were forced to give up the chance for a normal life with a husband and family in order to be part of the king's harem.

A "chosen-for-the-king" virgin spent a year in beauty preparations. Then on her special evening spent with the king, she could choose whatever she wanted to take and wear. The following morning she moved to a second harem managed by the eunuch Shaashgaz, and would never again return to the king unless requested by name (2:12-14). From our twenty-first century perspective, this treatment of women seems cruel—a total waste of women and their potential, but this was the culture of that day. As Protagoras, a philosopher of the time, stated: "Man [not mankind] is the measure of all things." This historical context makes the reality that God chose to use a woman to save His people all the more remarkable.

As Esther was taken away to begin her year of preparation, Mordecai warned her, "Do not tell anyone you are a Jew" (2:10). Mordecai feared that a Jewish girl would not receive kind or preferential treatment in the king's harem.[2] Esther obeyed Mordecai and left her home hiding her true identity. Esther made the choice to obey the authority figure in her life, Mordecai.

One of God's gifts to Esther was her beauty. We can also assume that she had a sweet, kind spirit because people immediately liked her. From the first day she arrived at the palace, Esther became the favorite of Hegai, the eunuch in charge of all the women. Hegai immediately ensured Esther had the best rooms, seven maids, and her beauty treatments began immediately. To keep in contact with Esther, Mordecai walked each day in front of the building where the king's harem was kept to learn of her activities and fate. Although God's name appears nowhere in the book of Esther, we see His guidance and direction of Esther's life.

After a year or more of waiting and preparing, Esther was given her night with the king. Before going to see King Xerxes, she sought the advice of Hegai on what to take and what to wear. Based on his recommendations, she went to the king and spent her night.

In true fairytale fashion, the king immediately fell in love with Esther, placed a crown on her head, and made her queen in Vashti's place. In verse 20, we are once again reminded, *"But Esther had kept secret her family background and nationality just as Mordecai had told her to do, for she continued to follow Mordecai's instructions as she had done when he was bringing her up."* Esther continued to allow someone else to think for her and tell her what to do.

The chapter closes with Esther obeying Mordecai's directions and reporting to the king about an assassination plot on his life that Mordecai overheard. The report was investigated and found to be true; thus Esther and Mordecai saved the king's life. The incident was recorded in the king's book of records, and then forgotten.

The Jolt (Esther 3 and 4)

By chapter 4 of Esther, a sharp contrast has developed between the world of Queen Esther and the world of Mordecai. The queen lived in the sumptuous palace away from the everyday concerns and worries of life. Mordecai, on the other hand, had torn his clothes and was sitting in front of the king's gate in sackcloth and ashes because of the decree sent from the king under Haman's direction that all Jews were to be destroyed and killed on the thirteenth day of the twelfth month (3:13). Mordecai felt partly responsible for the decree because of Haman's hatred and anger towards him.

When Esther received word that Mordecai was sitting at the gate in sackcloth and ashes, she was distressed, but clueless about the king's edict. "What could possibly be wrong with Uncle Mordecai?"

17

she wondered. She sent him a gift of clothes, which he refused. Next Esther sent her personal guard, Hathach, to Mordecai to learn the reason for his strange behavior (4: 5).

Mordecai informed Hathach about what was happening and sent a copy of the edict ordering the murder of all Jews throughout Persia—in essence, genocide. He instructed Hathach, *"Show this to Esther and explain what it means. Ask her to go to the king and beg him to have pity on her people, the Jews!"* (4:8, CEV). Up until this time Mordecai had been very specific that Esther was to keep her heritage a secret from the king. Now in a moment of extreme danger, Mordecai referred to the Jews as *her* people.

In the past, Esther obeyed Mordecai without question or comment. When he suggested she tell the king about the assassination plot, she responded positively to Mordecai's instructions (2:22). Times have changed.

Esther sent word back to Mordecai that the king had not requested to see her for thirty days. Esther was not feeling confident and self-assured in her relationship with the king. Next, she reminded Mordecai of the rules of the Persian court. In approaching the king uninvited, she was risking her life (4:11). No one—not even the queen—was allowed to approach the king without a summons. If an uninvited individual chose to approach the king, she or he would only live if the king chose to extend his gold scepter.

Mordecai answered Esther directly: *"Do not think that because you are in the king's house you alone of all the Jews will escape. For if you remain silent at this time, relief and deliverance for the Jews will arrive from another place, but you and your father's family will perish. And who knows but that you have come to royal position for such a time as this?"* (4:12-14).

18

Crisis and tragedy are often where leadership is forged. "Far from being a formula to learn," write Harold Myra and Marshall Shelley, "leadership is a set of life experiences melded by intense heat."[3] In the moment of crisis, Esther found her voice. She moved from a young woman who simply did what she was told to a mature woman who made choices. She was thinking, taking a risk, and choosing her voice. Esther became the woman God intended her to be.

The Result

In facing her defining moment, Esther was forced to choose her identity either as a woman of the pagan king's court, or a woman in covenant with God and His people. In her choice, she was transformed from the compliant woman who accepted life and did what others said into a leader of action who made things happen. She sent instructions back to Mordecai: *"Go, gather together all the Jews who are in Susa, and fast for me. Do not eat or drink for three days, night or day. . . . When this is done, I will go to the king, even though it is against the law. And if I perish, I perish"* (4:16). Esther as a true leader did not choose to act alone; she engaged others in the process allowing them to share in the success or failure.

After the three days of fasting concluded, Esther, knowing that her actions could cost her life, approached the king. Scripture records that the king was pleased to see Queen Esther and extended to her the gold scepter. We can assume during the three days of fasting, Esther was praying and preparing a plan to save her chosen people.

When the queen approached the king, he offered to give her up to half his kingdom. Her only request was that he and Haman come to a dinner that she would prepare. That evening at the dinner, the king again asked what Esther wanted. She requested that the following evening the king and Haman return to a second dinner she would fix for them.

During the second dinner, the king for the third time asked Esther, *"Queen Esther, what is your petition? It will be given you"* (7:2).

This time Esther was ready to reply. *"If I have found favor with you, O king, and if it pleases your majesty, grant me my life—this is my petition. And spare my people—this is my request. For I and my people have been sold for destruction and slaughter and annihilation"* (7:3-4).

The king was dumbfounded. *"Who is he? Where is the man who has dared to do such a thing?"* (7:5).

"The adversary and enemy is this vile Haman" (7:6), replied Esther.

The king became so angry at this information that he left and walked out into the garden. Haman, meanwhile, fell across Esther's couch begging her to spare his life. The king returned and ordered that Haman be hung (7:7-10).

In order to save the Jews from Haman's plot, the king granted Esther and Mordecai permission to write a new law, which allowed the Jews to defend themselves and defeat their enemies. The occasion is celebrated each year even today in Jewish families as the Festival of Purim.

Esther as a Leader for God

Esther is a woman empowered by God to lead. In Esther's life, we clearly observe all three of the leadership components of the Free-to-Lead model described earlier in the book: authentic leadership, strengths-based leadership, and servant leadership.

First, when her people are threatened with genocide, Esther chooses to become a leader revealing her authentic self. At the defining moment in her life, she moves from being a woman within the king's harem who hid her true identity to a woman who boldly claims to the king that she is a Jew. In her moment of crisis, she stands courageously as the Jewish woman she authentically was. In her leadership moment, she leads as her true self. Leadership always requires us to be our authentic selves—not copies of someone else or an imposter.

Second, Esther focuses as what she can do—not on what she can't do. As a leader, she utilizes her God-given gifts. Esther possessed the gifts of beauty, intelligence, and kindness. These were the gifts she used in winning the heart of the king and ultimately helping to save her people. Esther's plan demonstrates patience and wisdom. She didn't just go to the king and tell him Haman was plotting to kill her and her people. The king may not have believed her. She strategically and wittingly built intrigue within the king's mind as she made him wait before telling him her request. By inviting Haman to the dinners, she set a trap for her enemy. When Esther finally revealed the truth to the king, Haman revealed his guilt, and the king was furious enough to condemn him to death.

In the story, we also observe Esther's servant leadership. She leads in order to protect others. Her passion is to protect her people. Based on her passion, she acts by risking her life and going before the king. As a leader, she chooses not to act alone. She serves her people by providing the opportunity for them to be part of the solution. Mordecai and the Jews in the city fast for three days for the queen. Leadership author, Donald Phillips, writes that leadership involves "caring, inspiring, and persuading others to act for certain shared goals."[4] Esther led by inviting her people to participate with her by fasting and then providing them the opportunity and inspiration to defend themselves against their enemies.

21

My Response to Esther's Story

As I observe Esther's story, I see a woman God is empowering to save His people. Esther is not the quiet, submissive woman Pastor C told me I had to be if I wanted to serve God. In her story, we find a brave, decisive, courageous woman in her moment of crisis who chose to act in order to save her people. Esther's action was so important that even today she is celebrated in the Feast of Purim.

Esther teaches us that God wants to use you and me—His daughters—for His purpose to lead others. As you consider Esther's life and compare it with your own, where is God giving you the opportunity to be a voice for Him? I know today that God has given me a voice through my writing to tell other women how He wants to empower us to lead. He has given you opportunities also. He has given opportunities to both His sons and daughters to speak His message of love and truth.

Leadership Secrets from Esther

1. A leader knows God can overcome any childhood tragedy she endured.
2. A leader uses her God-given gifts such as beauty, intelligence, hospitality, motivation, organization, etc., for His glory.
3. A leader looks for the opportunity to use her voice for God.
4. A leader doesn't hide behind a mask; she presents herself as the authentic individual God created.

Just for YOU

Be Still and Listen to What God Is Saying to You
- When did you feel you were without a voice or hiding behind a mask? How does God feel when you hide who you really are?
- What are some of the defining moments in your life? How did you respond? What did you learn about you? What did you learn about God?

Write
As we begin our journey into seeing how God empowered women throughout the Bible to lead, you will find it helpful to answer in writing the following three questions:
- Authentically at your core, who are you?
- What gifts and strengths has God given you?
- Who do you want to serve? Where is your passion?

Do It Now
- Use your voice today. Share with one friend what you believe God is calling you to do. Ask that individual to pray for you as you begin this journey of allowing God to empower you.

CHAPTER TWO

A WOMAN WITH A PLAN: RAHAB

Joshua 2:1-24

Life isn't about finding yourself;
It's about creating yourself.
So live the life you imagined.
Henry David Thoreau

I am an individual who always had a plan—a plan for my life, a plan for my marriage and family, a plan for my ministry. My vocational plan was to be a minister's wife, so I married a preacher boy who was also a student at Moody Bible Institute. We moved down to Dallas, Texas from Wisconsin so he could attend Dallas Theological Seminary (DTS). After graduation, he joined the pastoral staff of a Bible church in Dallas. We were blessed with two beautiful children. We purchased a home, and for two years, all my dreams were fulfilled.

Then in the fall of 1982, my husband left the ministry. Thus ended my plan for my life. I was angry—angry at my husband ... angry at God. How was I to fulfill my calling in life to be a minister's wife? Was being a minister's wife even a legitimate calling? I wondered.

When I was honest with myself, I was also very frightened. How would we meet all our financial obligations and pay our bills?

During this time, I came across the words by Robert Louis Stevenson, which I adopted as my life statement:

To be what we are,
To become what we are capable of becoming,
Is the only end of life.

To be me authentically, how exciting would that be? What was I really capable of becoming? I did not know. I would need to walk this journey called life to find out the answer to that question.

I gave up planning my life. I gave up my small box that I had labeled "Possibilities," and traded it in for a blank slate as big as the universe on which God had written "Infinite Possibilities." God created me to be so much more than I could ever imagine. I chose to let go and let God allow me to be me—the "me" He created with all my special gifts and talents, idiosyncrasies and shortcomings.

Since the family's income was cut in half with my husband's new job and his departure from the ministry, I chose to act—to look for part-time employment. I read all types of books on careers and life choices. I came across a book on the advertising agency. As I read the descriptions of the various positions, I decided I wanted to be a copywriter. Writing is my gift; I have always loved to write.

I mentioned my desire to an acquaintance at church. Unbeknownst to me, he was the vice president of an ad agency, so he suggested I come and talk to him and his partner. The agency was small, so both my friend and his partner had the time to teach me the business. Most of the company's clients were Christian not-for-profit agencies like World Relief and SIM, formerly the Sudan Interior Mission. Before long, I was writing direct mail appeals to help feed children in Africa, build wells in Mali, and spread the Gospel of Christ around the world.

The hardest part of my career was leaving my children every day. David was five and in kindergarten. Heather was only two. I spent the morning with the kids, and then at 11:30, I took David to school and Heather to the daycare center. She often cried when I dropped her off, so I often cried all the way to work. The experience broke my heart. I believed mothers should be fulltime, stay-at-home moms, but I wanted to help support my family. I did not understand what God was doing in my life, but I knew I was walking through the doors He was opening and becoming much more than I had dreamed or planned.

Years later I met another woman in the pages of scripture who also faced the fear of the unknown. Her city was besieged by an enemy who was camped on the opposite side of the River Jordan at Shittim. As the rumors began to spread through the city of Jericho, fear and terror gripped the hearts of the inhabitants immobilizing them and gnawing away at whatever courage they might still possess. Rahab was a citizen of Jericho, but unlike the others, fear did not immobilize her. She was a prostitute. In her line of work, she learned to make fear a friend. When she sensed things were wrong, she knew she needed to act. Things were very wrong in Jericho, but what could she do?

Meeting Rahab

I am excited that God included the story of Rahab in the Bible. She is clearly not a saint. In fact, we could label her as damaged goods—a SINNER in capital letters. Scripture in referring to her in Joshua 2:1 uses the Hebrew word, *zonah,* which is translated as harlot, whore or prostitute. Yet, this is the person God chooses to help save His people. Rahab is one more woman throughout history empowered by God to lead. The message I hear loud and clear is that if God chose to use Rahab—a woman with a wanton past, He could also choose to use me and you.

The Context

The story opens when Commander Joshua sent out two spies on a covert operation with the instructions, *"Go, look over the land, ... especially Jericho"* (Joshua 2:1). God had already promised the land to the children of Israel, but Joshua was doing what was humanly possible to ensure success. As the Old Testament scholars, C. F. Keil and F. Delitzsch explain, "The help of God does not preclude human action but rather presupposes it."[1] As business pioneer, Mary Crowley, used to teach her salesforce of 38,000 women: "You pray as if everything depends on God, and act as if everything depends on you."

Over forty years have passed since the children of Israel left Egypt under Moses. Moses died, and in his place, Joshua was chosen by God to lead the army of Israel to enter the "promised" land. In preparation for the march into Canaan, Joshua sent out two spies on a reconnaissance mission. The spies entered the house of a prostitute with the hope of not being seen, but the city was on "red" alert. Everything was watched and reported. The stealth spies were noticed, and the king informed (2:2).

Rahab was a businesswoman who understood Jericho was in great peril. She had heard the stories about the Israelites from various male visitors to her establishment throughout the past several years, and she knew they were true. But it was not the people of Israel, however, that made Rahab afraid; it was their God, Yahweh. Rahab understood intuitively that Yahweh would win this battle. Somehow Rahab needed to find a way to save herself and her family. The question was: How?

When two strangers entered her house seeking lodging, she recognized her chance. Sensing the potential for danger, Rahab took the men to her roof and hid them under the flax she was drying (2:4, 6). Rahab soon received a message from the king, *"Bring out the men who came to you and entered your house, because they have come to spy out the whole land"* (2:3).

Rahab's Defining Moment

Rahab confirmed the truth that two men did indeed come to her, but she then spent the next several minutes telling the king's men three boldface lies. First, Rahab stated that she did not know where the men came from. Second, she explained the men had left. Finally she commented that she did not know where they had gone (Joshua 2:4-5). She then encouraged the king's men to go quickly toward the river so they could overtake the spies. Rahab chose to act in the face of fear to protect herself and her family. She chose to put her faith in the God of Israel.

But what about the lies she told? Is lying ever right? Biblical scholars and Christian ethicists wrestle with these types of questions regularly, and hold one of three positions related to Rahab's lie.

1. Conflicting absolutes. The Christian recognizes the two absolutes, sins and asks for forgiveness.
2. Hierarchical value. The Christian assigns a hierarchical value to the two absolutes and then chooses the higher good without sinning (cf. Matt. 23:22-24).
3. Non-conflicting absolutes. There must always be a third way.[2]

In life, you and I are responsible for the decisions we make, but God is available to provide guidance and wisdom for us. My personal belief follows the idea of hierarchical value from the list above. When it comes to the choice of saving a life or telling a lie, in my value system, it is more important to save a life. Rahab chose the higher good when she chose to tell a series of lies in order to protect the lives of the spies.

Unfinished Business

After the king's men left, Rahab returned to the rooftop and her guests. She risked her life to save these men, and now she presented her case requesting their protection for herself and her family.

I know that the Lord [Yahweh] has given this land to you and that a great fear of you has fallen on us, so that all who live in this country are melting in fear because of you. We have heard how the Lord dried up the water of the Red Sea for you when you came out of Egypt, and what you did to Sihon and Og, the two kings of the Amorites east of the Jordan, whom you completely destroyed. When we heard of it, our hearts melted and everyone's courage failed because of you, for the Lord your God is God in heaven above and on the earth below. Now then, please swear to me by the Lord that you will show kindness to my family, because I have shown kindness to you. Give me a sure sign that you will spare the lives of my father and mother, my brothers and sisters, and all who belong to them, and that you will save us from death (2:9-13).

In reviewing Rahab's monologue, several points become evident. First, she acknowledged that Israel's God, Yahweh, had given the land to the Israelites. It is remarkable that a woman who was raised in a polytheistic society was ready to accept the one true God. Second, she attested to the stories the Canaanites had heard about how the God of the Israelites dried up the Red Sea as they fled from Egypt and how He destroyed the two Amorite kings. Third, she revealed the Canaanites' fear of the Israelites because of their God who is both in heaven above and on the earth below. Finally, she asked the spies to ensure the safety of her family because she showed kindness to them. The spies promised to treat her and her family kindly and faithfully when God gave them the land, provided Rahab did not reveal the business of the spies to others (2:14).

God's Plan

As the Israelites were about to leave Rahab, we see that the omniscient God was in control of the story all along. The house of the harlot the spies randomly selected was built into the wall of the city. Not only had God prepared Rahab's heart, but an escape route. Rahab gave the men some final instructions and they affirmed their agreement to one another. The men then used one of Rahab's windows and a red cord to escape and were immediately outside the city wall (2:15).

Before the spies left, I can imagine Rahab grabbing the hand of the spokesman and shaking it vigorously to seal the deal. Scripture records that this woman of faith *"tied the scarlet cord in the window"* (2: 21). The two spies followed Rahab's instructions and returned to Joshua after hiding for three days in the mountains. They reported to Joshua, *"The Lord has surely given the whole land into our hands; all the people are melting in fear because of us"* (2: 24).

The story of Rahab and Jericho concludes in Joshua 6:22-25 when Joshua sent the two spies into Jericho to rescue Rahab and her family as they promised. We are told that Rahab and her family continued to live with the Israelites *"because she hid the men Joshua had sent as spies to Jericho"* (6:25).

30

Rahab as a Leader for God

From a human perspective, Rahab, as a Canaanite prostitute, seems an unlikely prospect as a leader for God; and yet, God chooses her. She demonstrates for us two key points concerning serving God from a leadership perspective. First, leadership is open to everyone — especially when we are serving God, because it is God who is empowering you and me to lead whether we are male or female, young or old. Second, God can overcome any past tragedies, traumas or mistakes, and use you or me for His purposes. Nothing you or I did — or had done to us — can make us unusable by God.

Next Rahab, as a leader, takes action even in the face of danger to herself. She practices courageous leadership. Her actions are driven by her love and concern for her family, and her willingness to act in the face of fear. Based on the Free-to-Lead model, Rahab models servant leadership. She acts to protect the spies by hiding them up on her roof. She stands up to the king's men and misdirects them in order to provide time for the spies to escape. She is aware of the concerns of others and informs Joshua's spies that the Canaanites fear the Israelites and their God. Her message encourages the secret agents and positively colors their report to Joshua. Finally, she secures a promise of safety for herself and her family when the Israelites attack her city. Rahab's kindness and leadership provide her with the opportunity to provide protection for her family.

My Response to Rahab's Story

As I examine this biblical record, I celebrate the fact that God chose Rahab as a leader. Her story is recorded not only here in Joshua, but the author of Hebrews includes her in his list of the faithful along with men like Abraham, Jacob, Joseph, and Moses. *"By faith, the prostitute Rahab, because she welcomed the spies, was not killed with those who were disobedient. And what more shall I say?"* (Hebrews 11:31-32). James also refers to her in his discussion about works and faith when he writes, *"In the same way, was not even Rahab the prostitute considered righteous for what she did when she gave lodging to the spies and sent them off in a different direction? As the body without the spirit is dead, so faith without deeds is dead"* (James 2:25-26). The reality that God empowered Rahab to become a leader for His people allows me to feel more comfortable with the reality that God wants to use me as a leader to make a difference for Him. How do you sense God empowering you to lead today? Rahab demonstrates that God does empower women to be part of His purpose and plan.

In Rahab's story, I also see that God is in the details of life. He goes before the spies in preparing Rahab for their visit. Rahab's home is located on the city walls allowing the spies an easy escape, and a way to mark Rahab's home when the Israelites return to conquer Jericho. One of the things that encourages my heart is to observe how God continues to work through the everyday details in my life. Where do you see Him working through the details in your life?

Leadership Secrets from Rahab

1. A leader knows God empowers both men and women to accomplish His purpose.
2. A leader possesses the courage to act even in the face of personal risks.
3. A leader believes God can use her no matter what her past when she is obedient to His guidance and direction.
4. A leader's action on behalf of her followers builds trust in her followers.

Just for YOU

Be Still and Listen to What God Is Saying to You

- Rahab was a woman, a prostitute, and a Canaanite—character-istics we might believe that would disallow her from serving God—especially in a leadership role. What past mistakes do you hold onto that you believe disqualify you from serving God? Are you ready to allow God to forgive you?

Write

- Identify where you sense God is empowering you to take an active role and lead—in your home, your church, your school, your job, or your community. What risks are involved?
- How will you find the courage to lead?

Do It Now

- Courageously take one action step today toward the opportunity where God is opening the door for you to lead.

CHAPTER THREE

SOMETIMES A WARRIOR: DEBORAH

Judges 4 and 5

She is clothed with strength and dignity;
she can laugh at the days to come.
Proverbs 31:25 (NIV)

*I*n the corporate environment of the ad agency where I worked, I began to thrive. I was writing—using my God-given gift. As my children grew older, I eventually began working fulltime. When the door opened for me to move from copywriter to account executive, I jumped at the opportunity. Soon I was managing the company's largest account, and was often the only woman sitting around the table at executive meetings with our clients. What I failed to notice was that there was another game going on that I did not understand or even realize existed—the corporate game. It was the mid-1980s when women were told: "To be successful, you must lead like a man."

There were books back then, and I read them all, that told a woman how to dress, how to wear her hair, how to open doors in order to succeed. As women in the business world, we were trying to break through what was called the glass ceiling. I came across the book that revolutionized my life and showed me the playing field: *Games Mother Never Taught You—Corporate Gamesmanship for Women* by Betty Lehan Harragan. I learned if I wanted a raise, I had to ask for it based on how much money I was making for the company. I realized if I wanted to be promoted, I must ask for the promotion. The rulebook I was raised on about being the nice girl where rewards simply fell from heaven, just did not lead to the success I wanted to achieve.

The underlying message of the corporate game was that life was not fair. I had to fight for what I wanted. I asked for a raise and I asked for a promotion. Soon I was making more money than I dreamed possible, but I felt at times I was split into two different people: the fighting "business me" and the loving "home me." The concept of leading from my authentic core—who I really was—never was part of the leadership equation I learned. I was encouraged to emulate the male model for leadership, "command and control," which often gets female bosses labeled with the "b" word. Unfortunately, I never questioned the leadership model I was taught. I wish back then I had been exposed to other options like "command and grace" leadership, which was modeled by a biblical woman who led with grace and kindness, even onto the battlefield.

Meeting Deborah

During the early 1980s, Mary Crowley was invited to speak to a group of over 1200 ministers in Memphis, Tennessee. As she looked across the sea of male faces, she asked these biblical scholars, "Who is Mrs. Lappidoth?"[1] The room fell silent. "Ah!" explained Crowley, with her typical kindness and grace. "You see, you know her as Deborah, because God calls a woman by her own name, not her husband's."

Deborah restarted my questioning Pastor C's position that women were to be quiet and submissive, and she quickly became one of my heroines. God placed her in a position of authority to be a voice for Him.

The Setting

We are introduced to Deborah in the book of Judges, which some Bible scholars suggest could better be called "The Book of Leaders." Judges 4:4 tells us that Deborah was a prophetess; she was the wife of Lappidoth; she judged Israel at the end of a twenty-year period when *"the Lord sold them into the hands of Jabin, king of Canaan"* (4:2). These were terrible times for the Israelites. Jabin's army possessed the improved technology of 900 chariots, which virtually left the Israelites powerless against him and his commander, Sisera.

Scripture tells us that Deborah received a message from God and so she summoned Barak, the head of the Israelite army. When he arrived, she excitedly told him the good news:

> *The Lord, the God of Israel, commands you: "Go, take with you ten thousand men of Naphtali and Zebulun and lead the way to Mount Tabor. I will lure Sisera, the commander of Jabin's army, with his chariots and troops to the Kishon River and give him into your hands"* (4:6-7).

Wow! A direct promise from God. Deborah expected Barak to be overjoyed. This was the type of opportunity most leaders only dream of. Finally after twenty years of oppression, God's silence was ending. He was ready to act on behalf of His people.

But Barak was less than ecstatic. In my mind's eye, I imagine he looked down at his sandals, like a little boy, when he replied to Deborah's announcement from God, *"If you go with me, I will go; but if you will not go with me, I won't go"* (4: 8).

"Really?" you may ask yourself, but that is Barak's response according to scripture!

Now, pretend for a moment, that you are Deborah. How would you respond to Barak's comment? Would you use "command and control," and berate him? Tell him to get his act together and get out on the battlefield?

Not Deborah. As a leader for God, she responded to Barak graciously without sarcasm and cynicism. She answered him in a manner, which protected his dignity: *"Very well ... I will go with you"* (Judges 4:9). She led with "command and grace," choosing not to assault Barak verbally or shame him because of his cowardly stance in the presence of overwhelming opportunity.

There was, however, a consequence to Barak's refusal to act without Deborah's assistance. God once again empowered women to accomplish His work.

Deborah stated to Barak, *"But because of the way you are going about this, the honor will not be yours, for the Lord will hand Sisera over to a woman"* (4:9). Not only did God use Deborah to deliver His message to the commander of the Israeli army, but God used Deborah to bring courage to the army. Furthermore, God would use another woman to kill Sisera, the Canaanite army commander. Sometimes God invites us as women to serve as warriors, leading with His authority and fighting with His courage.

The Battle

Barak, with Deborah by his side, positioned his men for battle up on Mount Tabor. When Sisera heard the news, he moved his men and 900 chariots to combat Barak. With the battle stage set, Deborah spoke to Barak, *"Go! This is the day the Lord has given Sisera into your hands. Has not the Lord gone ahead of you?"* (4:14).

So Barak with his ten thousand men moved to fight against the Canaanites. With God on their side, the Israelites won the battle, and Barak and his army pursued the Canaanite chariots and army until all died by the sword except Sisera.

The Victory

Sisera, the commander of the opposing army, sensed his army was losing the battle, so he abandoned his chariot and ran away from the fighting on foot (4:15). He then came to the tent of Jael, the wife of Heber, because the Canaanites had a peace agreement with the house of Heber (4:17-18). Jael greeted Sisera and invited him to hide in the tent instructing him, *"Don't be afraid"* (4:18). He accepted Jael's offer and entered the tent. When he asked for a cup of water to drink, she brought him a bottle of milk. When he laid down to rest, she covered him with a blanket. She went out of her way to make Sisera feel safe and protected. Sisera then instructed Jael to stand by the door of her tent. If anyone asked her if anyone was in her tent, she was instructed to say, *"No"* (4:20).

While Sisera was sleeping, Jael took a hammer and tent peg and drove the peg through his temple into the ground (4:21). She killed the commander of the Canaanites army! Then she left to find Barak and bring him into her tent where he witnessed the fact that Jael, a woman, killed Sisera (4:22). Through her action, Jael became one of Israel's celebrated heroines.

The Celebration Song

The story of Deborah concludes with Deborah and Barak singing a song of praise to the Lord in Judges 5, retelling how God won the battle. The following is the retelling of Jael's part in the victory beginning in verse 24 and concluding in verse 27.

> *Most blessed of women be Jael, the wife of Heber the Kenite; most blessed of tent-dwelling women.*
> *He asked for water, and she gave him milk; in a bowl fit for nobles she brought him curdled milk.*
> *Her hand reached for the tent peg, her right hand for the workman's hammer.*
> *She struck Sisera, she crushed his head, she shattered and pierced his temple.*
> *At her feet he sank, he fell; there he lay.*
> *At her feet he sank, he fell; where he sank, there he fell—dead*
> (5:24-27).

At the conclusion of the song, the author noted that peace reigned in the land of Israel for forty years. Deborah's and Jael's actions resulted in a generation of peace for the Israelite men, women, and innocent children of that time.

Deborah as a Leader for God

As I re-examine Deborah's story, I am immediately struck with the fact that unlike many of the Bible women we study in this book, Deborah is a woman who leads from a position of God-given authority. She is a prophet and a judge (Judges 4:4). As a prophet, she is a "mouthpiece for deity, a conduit for communication."[2] As a judge, she is viewed as a "deliverer" or "savior" of her people.[3] As God's servant, she is a leader who protects the people whom God entrusts to her: *"Deborah took command, protecting Israel as a mother protects her children"* (Judges 5:7, CEV). Through Deborah's leadership, we see God's Word emphasizing leadership from a feminine perspective—the nurturing, protecting love and care of a mother for her children.

Deborah does not, however, lead solely from her position of leadership. Position does not create leaders. She leads beginning with the authentic core of who she is with the "courage and spirit to make a significant difference."[4]

First as a leader, Deborah is willing and ready to respond when God calls. She demonstrates that she trusts God authentically from her innermost being. She appears in stark contrast to Barak who seems unwilling to trust God or to move forward without Deborah's presence. Deborah obeys God by communicating His message to Barak. Barak's response to God's message is his responsibility.

Second, she leads based on her strengths. We see the demonstration of her gifts of kindness, courage, and grace as she addresses Barak in his moment of weakness and then accompanies him onto the battlefield.

Third, her leadership is built on her passion and heart for the children of Israel. Courageously, as she stands beside Barak on the battlefield as a true servant leader, she emboldens the troops and inspires them to fight believing God will give them the victory.

Finally, she is a leader of action. She does not allow the fact she is a woman to restrict her actions, but goes right out to the battlefield and stands with Barak. At the end of the biblical account, Deborah continues to lead the Israelites through action by helping them sing and celebrate God's victory over the Canaanites through their willingness to fight. As leaders, we must remember to celebrate with our "followers" God's kindness and His blessings to us.

My Response to Deborah

Deborah is an encouragement to my heart. I see her in many ways as the quintessential female biblical leader. First, when God speaks, she acts. Deborah possesses a position of leadership and is involved in the daily activities of doing her job when God gives her a message. Immediately she responds to God's message. She is ready to lead.

Like Deborah, perhaps God has given you a place of authority to lead at work, in your community, in your church. Deborah chose to courageously stand up for God. Where is God giving you the position of authority where He wants you to stand up courageously and be a voice for Him to your world?

Secondly, from Deborah, I see a woman who leads authoritatively, but with grace, which can be translated "refined kindness." Deborah demonstrated "command and grace" leadership in her ongoing dealings with Barak. During my early years in corporate America, the idea of leadership and being feminine seemed incongruous. Leaders were to be "tough like men." Fortunately today, even leadership gurus are seeing the importance of both male and female leaders developing softer skills like nurturing and compassion.

Finally, Deborah's leadership made a difference for the people of Israel. God used her to help win the battle and usher in forty years of peace. How does God want to use you today? Are you listening to hear Him call you? Where is God asking you to lead? What difference can your leadership make for those around you?

Leadership Secrets from Deborah

1. A leader knows God calls her by her own name, not her husband's.
2. Leaders see that God places women, as well as men, in positions of authority where He expects them to lead.
3. A leader waits to hear God speak to her, so she can become a voice for Him.
4. Leaders are given the choice to obey or disobey God. There are consequences for disobedience.
5. A leader understands there are times she must be courageous.
6. A leader makes time to celebrate success with her "followers."

Just for YOU

Be Still and Listen to What God Is Saying to You
- Thank God for the positions of authority He has entrusted to you. Ask God to help you like Deborah reflect His love and grace as you lead.

Write
- Describe how you generally lead. How are "command and grace" demonstrated in your style of leadership?
- Scripture describes Deborah's leadership over Israel "as a mother protects her children." Write several ways your leadership reflects the love, care and nurturing of a mother.

Do It Now
- Identify one woman you can "stand beside" as she leads. What one thing can you do today to strengthen her as a leader? Do it!

CHAPTER FOUR

THE SHADOW OF DEATH:
MARTHA
John 11:1-44

Show up as you are, feeling what you are feeling.
Don't cover up your suffering.
If you're feeling anger or pain, bring your anger or pain.
But share it with the Divine and ask how to heal it.
Janet Conner

The phone was ringing ... ringing ... still ringing. It was pitch black in our bedroom. Who would call in the middle of the night?

My husband answered the phone and passed it to me. "It's your dad."

Suddenly I was awake. "Hey Dad, what's up?"

"Bob's dead. The plane he was flying crashed some time tonight. I don't know anymore. I'll call you in the morning when I have more details. I just wanted you to know." My dad hung up.

Numbly, I passed the phone to my husband. "My brother, Bob, just died in a plane wreck." My brother was a commercial pilot flying

43

small planes throughout the night, delivering documents for banks and other types of financial institutions. He and his wife were living in Ohio trying to pay off school bills before they became missionaries. Now—for Bob—there would be no tomorrows. He was dead.

My mind would not accept the words as reality. I was in classic denial. I did not fall apart. I did not react. I hit the PAUSE button and simply stopped so I could dissect the information a piece at a time until I could handle the facts—the reality.

I lay back down in bed. Tears began to stream down my cheeks. My little brother was dead. The words played over and over in my mind. Bob was four years younger than me. He had a wife—Glenda. Their two children were just innocent babies: a two-year-old daughter and a nine-month-old son. These babies would grow-up never even knowing their daddy. Still I couldn't believe or accept the reality. A loving God would not let this happen.

Morning finally arrived. I ached all over—like a bad case of the flu. I decided to go to work and simply pretend nothing had happened. I could not yet tolerate the reality, and I couldn't stay alone in my house doing nothing. I needed the busyness of my life to help me deny the truth. My brother was dead. Nothing I did would change that fact.

I was useless at work. That day I told only my boss about my brother's death. He had lost his brother several years before in an auto accident. Perhaps he could shed some light on my pain, but that was not to be. I knew immediately my boss still had some unfinished business related to his brother's passing.

The next few days passed as a blur. I learned Bob's memorial service was going to be in the small Ohio farming community where he and his young family lived. My mom suggested that my brother, sisters and I did not need to come for the service. I am not sure why. Perhaps she too was in denial. But we all needed to be there; and as the oldest child, I told my brother and sisters that fact. My brother Mark, my sister Marti, and I flew in from Dallas; my sister Barbara arrived from Chicago. We were all at the service to tell Bob good-bye.

Based on my family's strong religious background and belief that death was a homecoming, Bob's service was planned as a celebration led in part by my dad, who was a minister and had been for several decades. At the memorial service, I sat in my dark business suit on a cold, metal chair on the front row in a school gymnasium; the church my brother and his wife attended was too small for the expected number of guests. I was seething. A loving God, a kind God, my God did not kill daddies. God had not protected my little brother. Internally, I churned with the unfairness of my brother's untimely death.

As the service began, we were told to rejoice. Again and again, the words were proclaimed, "Bob is home with Jesus. Amen! Hallelujah!" But I wasn't celebrating. When everyone else in the auditorium said, "Amen," I said under my breath, "Oh shit." My relationship with the God of my father died that dreary afternoon. I cried out to God in my despair. And the answer to my prayers was a deafening, life-sucking silence. I not only lost my brother. I lost my God.

When I returned home to my husband and children, I remained angry at God. As a family, we stopped going to church. I chose to embrace my feelings honestly, authentically. A friend counseled me that I shouldn't be angry at God. But I was! If I chose to deny my feelings, who would I be fooling anyway? Me? God? He and I both knew the facts.

But it was in my anger that I kept searching for God and His truth. I wanted a God who was real and who accepted the real me with my doubts, my disbelief and my endless questions. I studied books about God that challenged my faith and thinking. I read my Bible, not as a textbook on dogma, but as a biography on God and Jesus. I wanted the love story where I could witness God loved the world. I continued to assure my worried friend that because God was truly God, I was safe even when I doubted. "Is God not stronger than my human doubts and questions?" I asked.

In my study of the Bible where I brought not only my head, but my pain, my emotions, my soul, I discovered a God who knew me and wanted me to know Him (John 10:14). Eventually, I also found another sister whose brother had died, and a God who loved her. In her brokenness, she was given a message not only to heal her pain, but to bring hope to all who have lost a loved one—including me. Her name was Martha.

Meeting Martha

The Setting (John 11)

The story of Martha is a story of relationships. Martha, Mary and their brother Lazarus were friends of Jesus—friends whom He loved (11:5). When the sisters sent word to Jesus that Lazarus was sick, they referred to their brother as *"the one you love"* (11:3). Curious isn't it, that the women did not ask Jesus to come and heal their brother? They simply wanted to make Him aware of the facts. Jesus loved their brother. Surely, He would not allow anything to happen to Lazarus.

Jesus did not act according to Mary and Martha's plan, however; and He waited an additional two days before traveling to Bethany. During that time, Lazarus died. Scripture tells us that Jesus then decided to travel to Bethany.

Based on my experience of losing a brother, I can imagine some of what Martha must have felt as she began her grieving process. Her brother was dead. Her beloved little brother was dead. The words played over and over in her mind. Still she couldn't believe or accept the reality. God would not; He should not; He could not allow this to happen to Lazarus. Jesus loved all three of the siblings too much. I can picture Martha sobbing once again. Her body ached all over. She was glad to allow Mary to sit in the middle of their home with all their friends who had come to comfort and console. But not Martha; she preferred her solitude. After all, she was the oldest, the one expected to be superwoman, and now she was falling a part.

Meeting Jesus

When Martha heard that Jesus was coming (11:17), she immediately hurried out the door to meet him while Mary continued to sit in the house. By this time, Lazarus had been in the tomb four days. As she reached Jesus, she cried out, *"Lord, ... if you had been here, my brother would not have died"* (11:21). Martha continued her monologue, demonstrating her faith in Jesus, *"But I know that even now God will give you whatever you ask"* (11:22). Based on her comment, I wonder if Martha hoped against reality that Jesus would somehow do the impossible and raise her brother from the dead.

The conversation continued and Jesus confirmed her hope. He gave her the answer she was seeking: *"Your brother will rise again"* (11:23). But Martha seemed unprepared to hear the answer to her prayer that Jesus was bringing her brother back to life now. Like us, she vacillated between her hope in God and the reality of her brother's death. She had created a box for her God based on what she believed was possible. She retreated into the intellectualism of her historical religious beliefs when faced with the possibility of a miracle pushing her hope into the future. *"I know he will rise again in the resurrection at the last day"* (11:24).

Then Jesus entrusted to this woman a God-size message, one of the fundamentals of our Christian faith and a basic truth of our theology. If we were creating a movie of this moment in the life of Christ, we would pause all action and sound. Silence would reign. Then the cellos would begin their low resonant sound. The kettle drum would join in providing a depth of drama with a low, slow "boom ... boom ... boom." As the rest of the orchestra joined in crescendoing to the musical climax, Jesus would speak: *"I am the resurrection and the life"* (11:25). So often, because the story is so familiar we miss to whom Jesus is speaking. We might assume this pillar of biblical truth was given to John, Peter or James. But Jesus presented this fundamental pillar of our faith to a woman.

Martha's Test

After entrusting Martha with this biblical truth, Jesus paused and asked her, *"Do you believe this?"* (11:26). It is at this point that Martha revealed the depth of her personal knowledge of Jesus—her personal confession of faith. *"Yes Lord, ... I believe that you are the Christ, the Son of God, who was to come into the world"* (11:27).

Martha's statement of faith is similar to the statement made by Peter, which is recorded in each of the synoptic gospels (cf. Mt. 16:16; Mk. 8:29; and Lk. 9:20). According to scripture, Jesus responded to Peter after his statement of faith by saying, *"Blessed are you, Simon son of Jonah, for this was not revealed to you by man, but by my Father in heaven"* (Mt. 16:17). How would Jesus respond to Martha? We will never know; because after her response to Jesus, Martha was on the move.

Martha's Retreat

Martha retreated to the security of her home after her spiritual high, and whispered to Mary that Jesus wanted to see her. *"The Teacher is here ... and is asking for you"* (11:28). The text indicates that Mary, hearing that Jesus wanted to see her, left immediately accompanied by a group of friends. We will read further about this Mary of Bethany later in the book. For now we will return to the story where we find Jesus, Martha, Mary and their friends going to the tomb of Lazarus.

Being Authentically Martha

When Jesus arrived at the tomb of Lazarus, He saw a large stone covering the opening and instructed that the stone be removed. Martha, in her take-charge manner, explained to Jesus that after four days, Lazarus's body was going to stink (11:39). I can just hear Martha saying, "Lord, this is not a good idea." Somehow Martha in her role as the ultimate hostess forgot about her earlier conversation with Jesus. If Jesus was going to raise Lazarus, the tomb needed to be opened, but Martha was not thinking logically. She was in overload trying to manage life in the midst of death.

Patiently Jesus addressed Martha and lovingly reminded her, *"Did I not tell you that if you believed, you would see the glory of God?"* (11:40). Jesus then raised His eyes to heaven and spoke, *"Father, I thank you that you have heard me. I knew that you always hear me, but I said this for the benefit of the people standing here, that they may believe that you sent me"* (11:41-42). Jesus then called, *"Lazarus, come out!"* (11:43). Lazarus emerged from the tomb bound in his grave wrappings.

The Bible story does not return to Martha, so we are left to imagine what took place in her life. Her despair of death was replaced with the joy of life. Her brother who once was dead now was alive. Martha witnessed firsthand and experienced at the soul level that Jesus was indeed the resurrection and the life.

Martha as a Leader for God

As I review this biblical account, I am awed by the fact that Jesus at this point and time chose to relay the theology of the resurrection to a woman. Why did He choose a woman? I think there are several reasons Jesus chose a woman leader for this critical task.

First, Martha is in the throes of grief experiencing the broken heart, the loss of appetite, depression, and extreme sadness. Death is not an academic topic to her; it is her experience and her reality.

Second, Jesus' personal death is only days away. He needed someone on the ground that He can trust to remember His truth, so He trusts Martha. Jesus knew His disciples would deny Him when the soldiers captured Him.

Third, Martha is about to experience God's resurrection in her life personally—the immediate exchange of sorrow for joy when Lazarus is resurrected. Martha's head knowledge that Christ is the resurrection and life is about to be translated by her heart and life into understanding at the soul level. Leading from the personal apex of tragedy is never easy. And yet it can be those times of crises when God reveals Himself giving us a message of hope that can encourage others. Martha lived through the despair of losing her brother. In several days, she will encourage the disciples as they lose their Savior, because she knows experientially that Jesus is the resurrection and the life.

My Response to Martha

Most of all I see in Martha's story a God who loves her who will walk with her through her crises. He is with her as she moves through the difficult times. I also see that God speaks to women entrusting them with His truths and allowing them to be a witness for Him. Martha is not sent away when the Teacher reveals theological truths. She is given the message of the resurrection at a time when she knows the reality of death.

In reviewing Martha's leadership in interaction with Jesus, I see a God who allows Martha to be her authentic self. As an individual, she is never asked to deny her feelings. She is patiently accepted where she is. She is not reprimanded when she doesn't understand how the message relates to her situation. She is entrusted with Christ's message of the resurrection; and through divine inspiration, she is able to reveal the truth about Jesus being the Christ (cf. Mt. 16:16). In witnessing Lazarus rise from the dead, Martha has an opportunity to close the circle of her learning and experientially understand Jesus' message to her.

Martha's future leadership role at the time of the crucifixion and before the resurrection is conjecture. But Martha has Jesus' word and her personal experience of death and resurrection to help enable others to act with hope and to encourage their hearts. Her words from Jesus as the resurrection and the life could encourage the hearts of the followers of Jesus during their time of greatest loss. What message has God given you to share with others based on your life's story?[1]

Leadership Secrets from Martha

1. A female leader knows God speaks to her as a woman.
2. A leader understands God wants her to be honest and authentic about her feelings toward God.
3. A leader experiences God's love and interaction based on who she is individually.
4. A leader has felt God's presence during her times of crisis and challenge.
5. A leader realizes God needs her to be His message bearer and share His truths with others.

Just for YOU

Be Still and Listen to What God Is Saying to You

- God promises, *"I will never leave you nor forsake you"* (Joshua 1:5). Like Martha, many of us take on the role of being superwoman or supermom. Where do you currently feel like you are internally falling apart? Where do you need to hear God's message of hope today?

Write

- Identify three to five of the most difficult times in your life, and list them on a piece of paper. Now spend a few more minutes identifying for each of those difficult times what you learned about yourself, and what you learned about God.

Do It Now

- Claim one of God's truths for you and your situation today. Ask God for what you need now. Remember you are God's precious daughter, and He loves you just as you are.

CHAPTER FIVE

PEACE BEYOND UNDERSTANDING: MARY, THE MOTHER OF JESUS

John 2:1-12

Whatever you can do or dream you can, begin it.
Boldness has genius, power and magic in it.

Goethe

y husband and I sat at the dinner table, enjoying the afterglow of a beautiful day in May. The kids were out riding their bikes around the neighborhood. Everything was perfect and at peace.

Suddenly a stranger was at our front door pounding and yelling—desperate for help. My husband and I jumped up and ran to answer.

"Your son's been in an accident. He's lying at the bottom of the creek at the end of the street."

Immediately, my husband ran out the door with the stranger. I called 9-1-1, and then took off. Soon sirens were blaring. I ran down into the ravine to be with my son. David was lying on his back at the bottom by the creek. He looked like a crumpled rag doll someone tossed away. He was alert, but he wasn't moving. The fire truck and

53

ambulance arrived at the scene. With the emergency personnel in the creek, I moved to the top of the hill where my daughter, Heather, was standing. We stood holding onto each other watching. A group of strangers began to gather around us.

Dave was strapped to a stretcher. The men lifted him out of the creek and into the ambulance. My husband accompanied my son, while Heather and I drove to the hospital in the car. In the Emergency Room we learned the worst: Dave was paralyzed from the neck down. Numerous x-rays were taken, but no breaks were visible. He was not hemorrhaging. The orthopedic surgeon would arrive in the morning and meet with us. Dave was sedated and placed in a hospital room. Nothing could be done until the morning. "Go home," we were told. We went home.

I arrived back at the hospital shortly after 7:00 a.m. My son was immobile. The orthopedic doctor arrived, checked Dave, and said we were going to do nothing. We were going to wait. My son fell back to sleep. Dave was only eleven. What could we do?

As I sat all alone in the hospital room watching my son at rest, God's peace simply washed over me. At that moment, I made the conscious decision to totally trust God—whether Dave was going to be physically okay or confined to a wheelchair for the rest of his life. He and I were going to be okay. God's grace was sufficient. I was experiencing the supernatural peace of God—God's gift because He loved me.

I had some firsthand knowledge of what it meant to be a quadriplegic. One of the artists, Chris, at the agency where I worked suffered a diving accident at eighteen. He had no movement in his hands or legs. Each day I watched Chris struggle, and I knew some of the price this hero paid to make a life on his own. I knew Dave was going to be okay no matter the outcome.

As I sat with Dave throughout the day, I learned more about how he ended up in the hospital. He had tried to jump his bike over the creek, and slammed into the opposite bank. Still we waited, but I was becoming impatient.

The second morning when the doctor came into David's room, I figuratively jumped the man and asked, "What are we doing here?"

"The body is designed to heal itself," the doctor patiently began. "We are waiting for the body to heal." Within five hours of the doctor's second visit, David began wiggling his toes. He was hungry. He wanted a pizza, not hospital food. As I watched my little boy move, I realized I was observing one of God's miracles. Within 48 hours, David was totally fine. He was back on his bike in three weeks; his only "scar" is a one-inch patch of white hair on the top of his head.

My experience with David became a life marker—my indicator for measuring life's experiences. For me when a "traumatic" situation arises, I simply come back to Dave's experience and ask myself, "Is this really a crisis?" Most of the time, the answer is "No." In John 2, we meet another mother who faced her share of crises loving her little boy. She is Mary, the mother of Jesus.

Meeting Mary, the Mother of Jesus

The Context

The story begins with the mother of Jesus attending a wedding celebration (John 2:1). In this recollection of the miracle, Mary does not have a name—only the position of being the mother of Jesus. I imagine as Mary watched the bride and bridegroom express their love to each other, she remembered her betrothal to Joseph. Of course, Mary and Joseph never had their wedding celebration. God intervened with plans of His own.

As though it were yesterday, Mary could recall in her mind's eye seeing the Angel Gabriel standing before her, "You will bring forth a child," he stated.

"But how?" Mary had asked. She had been so afraid during those days. She still remembered the song she sang to give herself strength and courage. She firmly believed it was a song God placed in her heart as she began to comprehend Gabriel's message, *"My soul doth magnify the Lord, and my spirit hath rejoiced in God my Savior"* (Lk. 1:46-47, KJV).

Her biggest fear back then was Joseph's reaction to the news that she was pregnant. He was such a kind and godly man. How could she ever explain what had happened to her? But God had interceded and told him in a dream. All of Mary's worries were always taken care of. It was so much easier carrying her heart's secrets with Joseph around. Together they shared that horrible trip of 90 miles to Bethlehem with Mary very pregnant. It is no wonder Jesus was born earlier than she expected.

Finally when she realized the baby was coming and told Joseph, she remembered his frantic search for a place to give birth to God's Son. To this day, she still liked the smell of clean hay. The stable was the first place she found since they began their journey where she could be alone—away from people. There were worse things than having a baby in a barn.

Then when she thought nothing stranger could happen, this little band of shepherds arrived at the barn to see the Baby—her Baby. Mary had to laugh. At first she hid Him not knowing who these shepherds were and what they wanted to do to her tiny infant son. Then they explained. It was the angels again. Mary was learning to believe nothing was impossible with God. Whenever the unusual happened, she simply tucked the thought away in her heart where she could consider it over and over again. There were still so many remarkable, unexplainable things in her heart.

As Mary came out of her reverie and viewed the wedding couple, she realized just how much she missed Joseph since his death. He was the one person who knew and understood this special child who was entrusted to them, God's Son.

Across the crowd of people, Mary watched as Jesus entered the wedding celebration with His five new friends. "Disciples," He called them. Mary knew things were changing in her relationship with her son. Jesus cautioned her things would change, but she was not sure what that would mean.

The Problem

"Oh Mary, Mary," a voice behind her called through the sobs. It was Mary's friend, the mother of the bridegroom. She was almost hysterical.

"What is wrong?" Mary asked.

"They have run out of wine, and my son will be ruined. What can we do?" the distraught woman explained. In Jewish culture at that time, running out of wine was the height of rudeness. It would be a social disgrace that would never be forgotten.[1]

"I know someone who can help," replied Mary. "I will go and get Him."

Mary immediately found Jesus and explained, *"They have no more wine"* (2:3). The text does not explain why this need was Mary's concern, but for whatever reason, Mary identified the emergency and took action. She became a caring leader at the point of crisis.

Jesus gazed at her for a few seconds with a mixture of knowing, love and kindness. Mary saw it in His eyes. He was reaching out to her.

Then He spoke. *"Dear woman, why do you involve me?"* (2:4), He asked.

Mary immediately heard the difference. Perhaps she felt a twinge of sadness in her heart. He was no longer calling her, "Mother." Their relationship was changing just as He had told her. In His next words, He gently reminded her of His higher calling, *"My time has not yet come."*

Mary studied her Son for a moment. She was puzzled, and realized she did not fully comprehend what He was trying to communicate, but that was nothing new for her. She had been misunderstanding Jesus since she and Joseph left Him at the temple in Jerusalem when He was only twelve. Mary turned to the servants and gave instructions, *"Do whatever he tells you"* (2:5). And with her words, Mary became one of the first to demonstrate her true belief in the efficacy of Jesus' words.[2] She modeled her utmost trust and faith in Jesus.

The Solution

In describing Jesus' miracle of turning the water into wine, the author of the Gospel of John does not refer to Mary again. Center stage has moved to Jesus. Jesus told the servants to fill six water pots with water. The servants obeyed Jesus and filled them to the brim. Jesus then instructed them to take a sample of the water turned to wine and present it to the master of the banquet. After sampling the wine, the man acknowledged to the bridegroom that the wine was better than what was being served at the beginning of the feast (2:10). We are told in verse 11 that the purpose of the miracle was to manifest Jesus' glory and that the disciples believed in Him. Then Jesus went down to Capernaum to be with His mother, brothers, and disciples (2:12).

Mary as a Leader for God

From a historical perspective, during the time of Christ, a man's world was the world outside his home — the public arena. On the other hand, a woman's world was the private world inside the home. The wedding in Cana merges these two different worlds.[3] Mary's actions at the wedding were totally appropriate for the culture of her day.

Mary's leadership is about getting a job done. She is an action-based leader with a passion for the bridegroom and his family. First, she cared enough about the people involved to see a need. As mentioned earlier, having sufficient wine during a wedding feast in that day and time was extremely important. Scripture does not reveal how Mary and Jesus were related to the wedding couple, but the fact that they were invited to the wedding indicates some type of relationship. Second, Mary was aware of where the needed resources were. In Israel at that time, one could not go simply down the street to the local Tom Thumb or Kroger to get some extra wine. She knew where the power to solve the crisis existed. She turned to Jesus as the provider.

Third, Mary acted courageously becoming a catalyst for action. She took the need to Jesus and invited Him to become a part of the solution. Fourth, in turning to Jesus with this need, Mary handed over the problem and trusted Him to solve it. She did not stand over Jesus micromanaging the process. Mary demonstrated that she trusted her Son implicitly when she instructed the servants, "Whatever he says, do it." She did not know how Jesus would solve the problem, but she placed her faith in Him. Because of her belief in Jesus, He solved the problem, manifested God's glory, and the disciples believed in Jesus (2:11).

My Response to Mary's Story

Mary saw a need, and she chose to act. Rather than play it safe and stay in the background, she took a risk and got involved. That is what leaders do. They see a need and respond. Mary's leadership demonstrates that sometimes God allows us to be part of a solution when we act without authority, recognition or glory. The choice, however, involves taking risks. Often as women, if we want to make a difference, we must risk getting involved, claiming our voice, bringing problems and situations to the attention of others who have the power and authority to address the issue.

As you go through your day, what needs do you see that pull on your heart, your passion? Jane Addams, a pioneer of social work who won the Nobel Peace Prize in 1931, made the statement: "Who if not you? When if not now?" Leadership requires someone to step out courageously when she sees a need and take action.

Maybe God is inviting you and me to lead without authority and without recognition in order to make a difference in our world. It is a lesson the mother of Jesus demonstrated graciously.

Leadership Secrets from Mary, the Mother of Jesus

1. A leader senses the needs of others around her because she cares.
2. A leader must sometimes act without permission or recognition.
3. A leader demonstrates her faith in God by doing her part and then trusting Him to do the impossible.
4. Leaders, men and women, can take their problems directly to God because He listens.

Just for YOU

Be Still and Listen to What God Is Saying to You

- When you are quiet, whose needs and hurts do you sense? Bring those concerns to God and ask Him how He may want to empower you to help.

Write

- As you think through your family, friends, and acquaintances, who needs God to meet their concerns? Write your prayer to God asking Him to help that other individual or individuals. Pray your prayer out loud to God after you write it. Trust God to answer.

Just Do It

- Write or email the person or persons you prayed for today. Let them know you are thinking about them and praying for them. Your message will encourage their hearts.

CHAPTER SIX

DAMAGED GOODS: THE WOMAN OF SAMARIA
John 4:4-42

When the storms come, do not hide in a corner waiting for the
storms to pass; rather, learn to dance in the rain.
Virginia Green

As I came home from work, my husband met me at our front door. "We've got to go someplace and talk," he said.

"Okay," I responded curiously. This had never happened before in our twenty-five years of marriage together. It was dinnertime, but our kids, Heather and David, were now sixteen and nineteen. No one would starve. I put down my things, stopped at the bathroom, and I was ready to go.

My husband drove the two of us to Bob Woodruff Park ... an oasis of family fun. Here we took our son when he was only two to watch the launch of the hot air balloons. Our daughter at eight caught her first fish in the pond. We pushed strollers, rode bikes and took romantic walks throughout the system of trails, woods, and playgrounds. Now my husband stopped the car so we could overlook the park. I couldn't imagine what this conversation was going to be about.

He turned off the car and looked at me. "I filed for divorce today. I thought you would rather hear it from me than have someone deliver the papers to your office."

"What are you talking about?" I shrieked. "You've never told me you are unhappy in our marriage! We don't fight. What is going on?"

"I want out," he stated.

"I will fight you," I shot back. Then the feelings came.

Like a tidal wave, I was hit with shock, disbelief and fiery anger. I screamed ... got out of the car ... slammed the door shut. I tried to breathe. I felt nauseous. I couldn't catch my breath. I was swimming in a vast void of inky, dark nothingness, and I was drowning. Family was everything to me. Three weeks earlier we celebrated our twenty-fifth wedding anniversary. We were in the process of building the house of—if I am honest—my dreams, but my husband added his critical eye for detail. Everything was perfect. Or so I thought.

I do not know how long I stood immobilized outside the car. I do not remember our exchange of words. I had unplugged myself from the reality of the situation. It is what I do; the way I react to extreme stress. The experts call it dissociation. I could not handle my husband's announcement with the pain, rejection, hurt. I was afraid if I did not unplug, I might fall apart. And what would happen then? Would I ever be able to put the pieces of me back together?

Eventually, we drove home. My husband in his usual calm fashion told the kids we were having problems. I was sad. Heartbroken. Soul sick. Some part of me felt like it had died.

That night my husband and I went to bed in the same bed we had shared for many, many years. We didn't touch. There was an icy wall of silence between us.

The next day I flew off to Los Angeles to art direct a photo shoot and create a brochure for an inner city rescue mission. When I arrived, I checked into the hotel. The photo shoot would not begin until the next morning. I was grateful for my time alone in the hotel room where I could scream, beat the walls, and spend hours crying without a witness. And there was no one ... no one who needed me to be the "put-together" mom. I was in a safe place to fall apart. In every quiet moment when I was not performing some job, tears leaked from my eyes.

The following morning at the community center where the mission served breakfast, we began photographing the individuals helped by the mission—women without jobs ... without education ... and with children.

I will never forget one young woman. She was only nineteen with her two-year-old straddled on her hip. She wore black pants, a halter-top, and an open flannel shirt, which clearly revealed the fact she was about six-months pregnant. I couldn't help but sense the stark contrast between this nameless young mom and me.

As I conversed with this woman, I listened and I learned. She told me how the father of her two-year-old daughter left her before her baby was born. Now she was living with her boyfriend. She hadn't finished high school, but was hoping to get her GED with the help of the mission. This woman spoke of her future and that of her children—a future filled with hope.

In my mind, I heard God roaring like a lion, "What do you have to complain about? You are a professional woman with a job, a career, and an education. I will provide for you and your children because I love you." During the next three years, whenever I experienced moments of self-doubt and wallowed in self-pity, the image of this brave, courageous woman returned to me with God's message, "I will provide for you because I love you."

After eight months of counseling, prayer, and everything else I could think to try, our marriage ended. I will not share any further details. Marriage is a dance shared by two separate individuals, and both my husband and I failed to make our marriage work.

Unfortunately, divorce was not only difficult and challenging; in my religious circle, it was one of the condemning sins that labeled you as unfit to serve God in any capacity. After my husband moved out of our home, I felt marked by the failure of my marriage. I felt like I was damaged goods—almost as if I was now required to wear an imaginary letter "D" from a chain hanging around my neck. But I was soon to see that was not God's way.

In John 4, I met a woman who like me had lost a relationship with her husband—in her case, five husbands. Although the Bible does not label the woman as divorced, Bible scholars assume she was a woman of ill repute. She was living with a man to whom she wasn't married. She was so scorned by her community, that she chose to draw water in the middle of the day. Yet, in this woman, I discovered hope because Jesus demonstrated He cared about this woman.

Meeting the Woman of Samaria

Context

The story opens with Jesus travelling from Judea to Galilee by way of Samaria. He was tired, and so He stopped at about noon by Jacob's well outside the town of Sychar. His disciples went to town to buy food.

Scripture tells us, *"Now he [Jesus] had to go through Samaria"* (John 4: 4). Jesus had to go to Samaria for several reasons. First, He

65

needed to get to Galilee, and Samaria was the shorter of two routes to get Him to His destination. Second, Jesus wanted to demonstrate that the salvation He was bringing to the world was not just for the Jews, but also for the Gentiles and Samaritans. Third, there was a woman in Samaria who needed the living, satisfying water only He could supply. The first reason is practical; the second reason is philosophical; and the third reason is personal. You and I worship a personal God who is interested in what happens to us individually. Jesus went to Samaria because as Anne Graham Lotz puts it: Jesus had a divine appointment with a woman in need.[1]

In the Everydayness of Life

In the middle of the day, a lone woman approached the well of Jacob carrying a water jug. She preferred her solitude to the critical eyes of the townswomen who generally filled their water jugs in the morning and evening. She was tired of their relentless gossip and judgmental attitudes about her numerous husbands. She was lost in her own thoughts when a stranger called out, *"Will you give me a drink?"* (John 4:7).

The woman looked at the stranger. Many women of that day would simply comply to the man's request for water, but not this woman. She was shocked, but not cowered. *"How can you ask me for a drink?"* she boldly inquired. *"You are a Jew and I am a Samaritan woman"* (4:9). From a Jewish perspective, Samaritans were the "half-bloods" of the world—part Jew and part Gentile. They were considered unclean. Any self-respecting Jew would have nothing to do with a Samaritan or anything she touched.

The stranger overlooked the woman's brashness and responded kindly, *"If you knew the gift of God and who it is that asks you for a drink, You would have asked him and he would have given you living water"* (4:10).

Now the woman looked at the man with an incredulous stare. She moved from shock to disbelief. Here she was simply trying to draw water like she did every day. A Jewish man had asked her for water and now he was talking to her about a gift from God. What was happening?

Inwardly perhaps the woman thought, "God wants to give me something? Clearly this stranger has no idea who I am. I am damaged goods—divorced not once, but five times. God would want nothing to do with me."

The problem, however, was that this stranger spoke to the woman with dignity and respect. She was accustomed to judgmental, condemning talk. Kindness was one of the few things she couldn't handle—especially from a man, so she came back with fighting, arguing words.

She pointed out to Jesus the facts as she saw them. *"Sir, you have nothing to draw with and the well is deep. Where can you get this living water?"* (4:11). Then she moved to the strength of the town's history. *"Are you greater than our father Jacob who gave us this well and drank from it himself, as did also his sons and his flocks and herds?"* (4:12).

Jesus answered her questions by contrasting the water in the well with the living water He mentioned. *"Everyone who drinks this water will be thirsty again, but whoever drinks the water I give him will never thirst. Indeed, the water I give him will become in him a spring of water welling up to eternal life"* (4:13-14).

With that type of promise, this practical woman who was weary of daily trips to the well simply asked, *"Sir, give me this water"* (4:15). She put her faith in the stranger's message and asked for the gift.

An Honest Conversation

Jesus was concerned with healing this woman's brokenness, so He touched on her sore spot—the point where she internally condemned herself. *"Go, call your husband and come back"* (4:16), He instructed.

The woman responded as truthfully as possible, *"I have no husband"* (4:17).

Jesus commended her for her honesty, *"You are right . . . The fact is, you have had five husbands, and the man you now have is not your husband. What you have said is quite true"* (4:18). Jesus praised her for telling the truth. He demonstrated that He accepted her even with her past mistakes. But Jesus was getting too close for comfort, so the woman changed the topic turning the focus back on Jesus.

She stated, *"Sir, I can see you are a prophet"* (4:19). She then ensured the subject matter would stay away from her personal life by bringing up the age-old debate about where the Jews and Samaritans thought God should be worshipped (4:20). Jesus, as the master communicator, redirected the conversation back to His agenda.

A Divine Revelation

Jesus affirmed the woman's religious understanding by explaining that a new age was coming when worshipers *"will worship the Father neither on this mountain nor in Jerusalem. . . . Yet a time is coming and has now come when the true worshipers will worship the Father in spirit and truth"* (4:23-24). Throughout His lifetime, Jesus spoke to women revealing spiritual truths and affirming that women were an integral part of His spiritual kingdom.

The woman responded to Jesus' answer based on her current understanding, *"I know that Messiah (called Christ) is coming. When he comes, he will explain everything to us"* (4:25).

In what must have been a total earthshaking moment, Jesus responded simply and directly to this woman, *"I who speak to you am he"* (4:26).

Can you imagine what this woman thought? How she might feel? This man who kindly and respectfully discussed religion with her ... this man who somehow knew her sordid past ... this man just told her He was the Messiah, and He was speaking to her. What would you do?

The Samaritan woman was left with a choice. What would she do with the message Jesus entrusted to her?

The Woman's Response to God's Message

As the Samaritan woman struggled with her moment of destiny, the disciples returned to Jesus. Being steeped in the customs and traditions of their times, the disciples were concerned their teacher was talking to a woman in public. The disciples, however, lacked the courage to ask Jesus directly, *"Why are you talking with her?"* (4: 27). According to Jewish tradition, rabbis were discouraged from speaking to women about any theological issue, "liking the process of such intellectual discussion to liberating them or opening them to a life of immorality."[2] Based on His actions, however, Jesus did not allow the customs of His day to restrict His conversations only to men. In fact, throughout His ministry, Jesus did liberate women. His message was and is for everyone regardless of gender.

Scripture returns its focus back to the Samaritan woman who faced what leadership experts refer to as the "defining moment"—that point in time and space when an individual either chooses to act or not to act. The decision marks who one genuinely is at his or her core.

The Samaritan woman chose to act on the knowledge that the Messiah was conversing with her. Scripture records, *"Then, leaving her water jar, the woman went back to the town and said to the people,*

'*Come, see a man who told me everything I ever did. Could this be the Christ?*'" (4:28-29). With this message, the woman became the first missionary to the Samaritans.

The Woman's Wisdom

In her brief conversation with the townspeople, we observe the wisdom of the Samaritan woman. When she arrived in town, she told the people what happened to her. She did not give a theological discourse. She simply shared her story—her experience with Jesus. As she became a voice for God, she remained her authentic self.

If she had told the townspeople that this man was the Messiah, they would have argued and disagreed with her. Instead, she simply presented the town's leaders with an invitation to come and see the man who told her everything she had done. Then she asked them a question, "Could this man be the Christ?"

Now the city fathers had a reason to meet the man at the well. They had a responsibility to answer the woman's question. The text tells us that they came out of Sychar to meet Jesus.

The result of the woman's encounter with Jesus and her decision to be a voice for God to her community was that many people in her town believed that Jesus was the Savior of the world (4:42). God empowered this woman to become a leader for her people.

The Samaritan Woman as a Leader for God

In looking at leadership through the account of the Samaritan woman, I am reminded that leadership is for everyone. In the introduction of this book, we established that leadership allows people like us to bring out our best as we help lead others.[3] The Samaritan woman became so much more than she imagined through her experience with Jesus and her choice to act.

Leadership also demands we each begin at the core with who we are, our authentic self, including our past, our failures and mistakes. Researcher and writer Brené Brown writes: "Authenticity is the daily practice of letting go of who we think we're supposed to be and embracing who we are."[4] The Samaritan woman courageously met Jesus as herself with her knowledge of both her culture and religion.

The woman is also an action-based leader. She left her water jug and ran to town, because she had a message for the townspeople. The Samaritan woman revealed her servant-leadership heart when she told the town residents the story of her encounter with Jesus. As a wise female leader, she did not tell the town's leaders, "Jesus is the Messiah." She asked them, "Could this man be the Messiah?" Because of her authenticity, her actions, and her caring, the town came out to meet Jesus.

My Response to the Samaritan Woman

Every time I read this woman's story, I am encouraged that Jesus goes out of his way to meet a woman in the everydayness of her life. He is not requiring her to go to a synagogue or church; He is not asking her to be in an attitude of prayer. He is meeting her where she is. She is drawing water—something she has probably done every day of her life since she was a little girl. As I look at the love Jesus demonstrates in meeting this woman at the well in Samaria, I ask myself: Where is God trying to meet me? Am I practicing being present enough and in touch with the world around me to hear God speak to me in the everydayness of my life?

Her story reminds me also of the fact that God speaks to His daughters and desires to use us as a voice to communicate His message of love to others. The story of this nameless woman is preserved in Holy Scripture as a witness to the fact, according to the author of the Gospel of John, *"that Jesus is the Christ, the Son of God"* (John 20:31). The truth is Jesus spoke to women when He was on earth, and He wants to speak to women today. What message has God given to you?

Finally, I also see in this biblical account that Jesus chooses to speak to and empower a shamed, divorced woman. Because of my divorce, I became a more real individual. I stopped pretending and learned real humility. I felt like a total failure, and so I brought my brokenness to God and said, "Here I am if you want me." I practiced trusting and walking by faith. Perhaps there is something in your life that you believe disqualifies you from being of service to God. Are you ready to bring your brokenness to God and say, "Here I am"?

Leadership Secrets from the Woman of Samaria

1. A godly leader understands that God desires to speak to each of us—whether we are male or female.
2. A leader knows God speaks in the everyday events of life, so she looks for Him there.
3. A leader realizes God can look beyond her past mistakes and failures.
4. A leader encourages others by sharing what God is doing in her life. Being a biblical scholar, although useful, is not required. God needs the individual and her story.

Just for You

Be Still and Listen to What God Is Saying to You

- Jesus went out of His way to speak to the woman of Samaria. Pause and reflect on how precious you are to God. Can you sense His love? How is He speaking to you in the everyday-ness of your life? What is He saying?

Write

- Do you ever feel less than valuable or precious to God? Write what happened in your life that encourages you to feel broken or unworthy.
- Based on your life experiences, write out what message God has given you to share first with yourself, and then with others.

Do It Now

- Like the woman at the well, take one step and become a voice for God based on His message to you.

CHAPTER SEVEN

THE DARK NIGHT OF THE SOUL: MARY MAGDALENE

John 20:1-18

Before you can begin something new,
you have to end what used to be.
William Bridges

hile living through my divorce, I smashed the rosy-colored glasses I was given in childhood. Life was not pretty. I felt naked and vulnerable. All of my props were gone, and I cried out to God nightly. Once again I began experiencing life in the here and now. Sadness became my constant companion, and I cried continually. Of course, I got into therapy and worked with several professionals in order to help me heal the emotional pain in my life. I lost the compulsory ten pounds because of the divorce, plus ten more.

The first question I asked was: Does Jesus really care about me? I felt totally abandoned by God. I chose to return to church, but this time I chose a denomination different from the churches of my growing up years. In my work with nonprofit organizations, I found this particular denomination to be very accepting and forgiving. On my first Sunday at my new church, a female minister gave the sermon. Now I don't know how you feel about female ministers, but I can tell you how I felt that day. I sensed God saying, "I love you just as you are—a woman who is bright and intelligent and divorced. I will take care of you."

Through the next days, weeks, and then months and years, I learned to depend on God in what St. John of Chrysostom called the dark night of the soul. If something good was going to come out of the mess of my marriage, the strength had to come from somewhere besides me.

During that time, I learned to be still. I wrote in my journal a prayer: "I come with empty hands and open mind to find everything. The student is finally ready to learn from the Teacher. I will go to bed mindful of God and His strength."

God cares for you. God cares for me. Mother Teresa wrote, "The biggest disease today is not leprosy or tuberculosis, but rather the feeling of being unwanted." From another woman out of the pages of scripture, I saw a God who loves, trusts and cares for women.

Meeting Mary Magdalene

I met Mary Magdalene not in any Bible study, but in my new church on an Easter Sunday morning. The senior minister preached that year on Mary Magdalene's lack of faith because she refused to enter the tomb. As the congregation read together the scripture passage for the sermon from John 20:1-18, my heart was thrilled. I didn't see a woman without faith. I saw a God who cared so deeply for this woman in her pain that He stopped to speak to her—immediately replacing sadness with joy, despair with hope. This was the God who could heal my pain and hurt. This was the God I needed to know.

On that pew in church, I mentally tuned out the minister, a skill many mothers develop when their children are preschoolers. I didn't care what the preacher was saying. I wanted to know what God had to say to me. I began to look at the story in scripture and Mary Magdalene through a woman's eyes. What would God reveal to me as I searched God's Holy Word?

A Proper Introduction

The story begins on an early Sunday morning while the sky was still dark. Mary Magdalene arrived at the tomb, not because she didn't have faith, but because she was grieving. When she saw the tomb was open, she was frightened. Were there grave robbers in the area? She didn't enter the tomb because she was concerned about her safety. She ran back to where the friends and disciples of Jesus were staying and got Peter and John (John 20:2). The men hurried to the tomb, saw it was empty, and then ran off (20:10).

Mary Magdalene returned to the tomb, still grieving. She was quiet ... waiting. She stood present with her pain, and God met her there at her moment of hurt.

First she stooped, peered into the tomb, and saw two individuals dressed in white. They asked her, *"Woman, why are you crying?"* (20:13).

"They have taken my Lord away, ... and I don't know where they have put him." she responded (20:13).

Mary Magdalene stood, turned and saw another man who asked, *"Woman, why are you crying? Who is it you are looking for?"* (20:15).

At this point, Mary Magdalene gained courage. She wanted to protect the body of Christ. *"Sir, if you have carried Him away, tell me where you have put Him, and I will get Him"* (20:15). She was empowered by her tragedy. She wanted Jesus.

And then Jesus called her by her name—not Mary Magdalene— but simply, *"Mary"* (20:16). Jesus called her by name for one reason:

He loved her. If anyone should have been in a hurry, it was Jesus. He waited to ascend into heaven because one of His beloved children, a woman, was hurting. People are important to Jesus. And Mary needed to be assured. Her Lord and Savior was risen!

In the simple utterance of her name, Mary Magdalene immediately recognized the speaker. *"Rabboni!"* she uttered—"Teacher" (20:16), and grabbed Him.

How much time passed? Who knows? We are not told, but eventually Jesus told Mary that she needed to let go of Him because He needed to go and see His Father (20:17). Mary was then given one of the most important messages in the history of the Church, *"Go ... to my brothers and tell them, 'I am returning to my Father and your Father, to my God and your God'"* (20:17).

The Response

Mary responded to Jesus with obedience. She went to the disciples with her message, *"I have seen the Lord!"* (20:18). She became the message bearer—Christ is risen!

How did the disciples respond? In Mark's gospel, we read that when Mary Magdalene returned with Christ's message, they did not believe her (Mark 16:11). Mary Magdalene reported that she saw Jesus and touched the risen Lord, but they could not hear her. Eventually, Jesus Himself appeared to the disciples on Sunday evening. Then and only then did they believe He was risen (John 20:19-20).

A Further Look at Mary Magdalene

My original introduction to Mary Magdalene spurred me to learn more about this woman. Her name appears in all four gospels. Luke introduces her as one of the women who travelled with Jesus and His disciples when he writes: *"The Twelve were with Him, and also some women who had been cured of evil spirits and disease: Mary (called Magdalene) from whom seven demons had come out; Joanna the wife of Cuza, the manager of Herod's household; Susanna; and many others. These women were helping to support them out of their own means"* (Luke 8:1-3). Clearly, Jesus did not segregate Himself with His twelve disciples away in some cloistered retreat. He lived in the midst of people. He traveled with a group of men and women and included women in His ministry allowing them to see His miracles and hear His teachings.

Luke describes the uniqueness of these women. First, they were women who had experienced firsthand the healing of Jesus in their lives (8:2). They knew the power of God. Second, these women were given the incredible privilege of hearing and learning what Jesus was teaching the disciples—seeing firsthand the power of God in the lives of others. They became Christ's witnesses. Third, these women supported the ministry of Jesus with their personal resources (8:3). Giving to God was the response of their grateful hearts, rather than an obligation or duty.

Witness to the Death and Burial of Jesus

Mary Magdalene was not only an eyewitness to the miracles and teachings of Jesus; she was a witness to His death and burial. The authors of Matthew, Mark and John comment that many women who had ministered to Him observed the crucifixion from a distance including Mary Magdalene (Matthew 27:55-56, Mark 15:40-41, and John 19:25). When the disciples abandoned their Lord, these women including Mary Magdalene possessed the courage to stay with their Savior during His horrific suffering. Luke's gospel adds that these women observed the body of Jesus being taken down from the cross by Joseph of Arimathea and placed in a tomb (Luke 23:49-55). They saw where Jesus was buried. Early Sunday morning in the face of potential danger from grave robbers or soldiers, these women returned to His gravesite. They set aside their fears to honor what they thought would be the body of their Lord.

Mary Magdalene as a Leader for God

Mary Magdalene is a woman who leads from the sidelines without a formal position or authority. Based on the number of biblical references to Mary Magdalene, and her position within the lists of names, we can assume she was a leader among the women, but she had no official title (Luke 8:2-3).

Authentically, she personally experienced the power of Jesus when He healed her from the seven demons. She traveled with Jesus and the disciples, and heard His teachings and saw His miracles. From the core of her being, she modeled how the power of God can change a life.

From a strengths-based perspective, she led through her financial support of Jesus' ministry. She demonstrated courage in her willingness to stand where she could provide an eyewitness testimony to both the death and burial of Christ.

Her honesty and trustworthiness are revealed when Jesus entrusted her with the critical task of telling the disciples that He is risen. She demonstrated obedience and servant leadership when she delivered Christ's message of hope to the grieving disciples.

My Response to Mary Magdalene's Story

As I re-examine Mary Magdalene's story, I am struck by two major points. First, Jesus chose to reveal Himself as the risen Christ first to a woman. Second, Mary Magdalene is a woman in the major throes of chaos and change. She is a woman in transition.

Why Did the Resurrected Jesus Appear First to a Woman?

Until recently, I never thought of the significance of Jesus' choice to reveal Himself as the risen Christ first to a woman. I think back to my time ministering with my husband in Pastor C's church. If Jesus had been Pastor C, he never would have selected a woman. Pastor C believed women were to be silent in the church. But Jesus asked Mary Magdalene to carry His message of hope to the disciples. How have I missed this point for so long? Jesus chose a woman to witness His risen form—even before He had ascended to His Father or appeared to the eleven.

As I look at the passage today and celebrate the fact that God loves both His sons and daughters, I ask myself again: Why a woman? Why did Jesus choose to appear as the risen Lord first to a woman? But the question is even bigger: Why did Jesus include women in His earthly ministry? I came up with several responses, but my list is in no way exhaustive. Perhaps you can come up with several additional reasons.

First, Jesus included women because He wanted to demonstrate in more than words that He lived, died and rose again for the whole world—men and women—not just men. For hundreds of years, the Greek world believed and taught that man—not mankind—was the center of life. Jesus' words in John 3:16, "For God so loved the world, that He gave His only begotten Son," were revolutionary. Through His ministry, Jesus demonstrated by His actions that He included women and men, adults and children.

Second, Jesus included women because He wanted God to be seen from more than just a male perspective. God's Word reveals in Genesis that He created us in His image—male and female (Gn

1:27). As author Janet Davis writes, "Maybe women have a whole different way of experiencing God than men."[1] I agree. The Bible stories, especially of women, look very different when seen through the eyes of a woman. Today neuroscientists understand that men's and women's brains "produce equivalent intellectual performance, [but] their brains do it differently."[2]

Third, God chose to include women in His plan because He wanted to demonstrate that we as women, along with men, are His message bearers. Silence is not desired. As I re-examine scripture, I am amazed to see that God first entrusted to women two of the fundamental pillars of our Christian faith: the virgin birth, and the resurrection.

Mary, the mother of Jesus, was the primary witness to the virgin birth of Christ. Because the gospels were not written until twenty plus years after Christ's death as biblical scholars surmise, she was probably the only living witness to the details of the story including the manger, shepherds, and wise men.

As we saw earlier in this book, Jesus entrusted Martha with the theology of the resurrection when He gave her the message, "I am the resurrection and the life." To Mary Magdalene, Jesus entrusted the first revelation of the reality of His resurrection.

A Woman in Transition

Mary Magdalene is also a woman who was profoundly changed by her encounters with Jesus. From her initial healing, to living on the "ministry" road with Jesus and the disciples, to experiencing the heartbreak of Christ's death, and the joy of His resurrection, Mary Magdalene was a woman in transition. How do we as women survive change in our lives?

After my divorce, I was also a woman in transition, changing in order to put back together the pieces of my life. Through friends and relationships, God began healing the brokenness in my life. I asked myself the question: What do I want? The Bible says that when we delight in God, He will give us the desires of our heart (Ps 37:4), but sometimes we—especially as women—do not know what we want. Of course, the obvious answer for me was to be married to my ex-husband, but that thought only led to more tears. I always held onto the hope that God in His infinite power would reunite my husband and me; but after my husband remarried, that seemed a rather unlikely prospect. I moved on.

What did I want? I began making my list. I wanted my PhD. I wanted to travel. I wanted to have people back in my life. I wanted to be happy again. And I did want to marry again. I learned to be honest with what my heart and my soul told me I wanted.

Piece by piece, I was changing. My kids saw it. My friends saw it. After awhile, even I saw it. During my change experience, I came across four rules on how to change.[3] In analyzing the rules, I saw they applied to Mary Magdalene as well as to me. I want to share them with you because I found them so helpful in enabling me to survive change.

Rule One. Show up. Too often we miss opportunities and the potential to be leaders because we are afraid of failing, so we do not show up. Mary Magdalene arrived at the tomb. You and I need to show up when God opens a door for us.

Rule Two. Be present. If you are going to show up, be willing to give it your best and be present. Mary Magdalene engaged in conversation with both the angels in the tomb, and the man she assumed to be the gardener. She was present. We need to be present when God gives us opportunities to lead, to grow, and to change.

Rule Three. Tell the truth. Too often, we fall into the trap of saying what we think we are supposed to be saying. When all the rules seem to be up for grabs, go back to the basics: tell the truth. Many seemingly insurmountable problems can be transformed when someone finally tells the truth. Mary Magdalene told the disciples the truth: Christ is risen.

Rule Four. Let go of the outcomes. For some of us, it is tempting to do our best and then manipulate the outcome. Transitions and changes are generally out of our control, so let go and go with the flow. When Mary Magdalene was sent by Jesus to deliver His message to the disciples, she obeyed, and then let go. Her task was to deliver the message, not to argue with the disciples.

Perhaps you are in a season of change in your life. One of God's strongest tools of ministry is the personal story, especially stories of how God worked in your life and mine to change us revealing our authenticity and vulnerability. How is God working in your life to change you? Do you sense His love and care? From Mary Magdalene on that Easter Sunday morning, God reminded me once again that He loves me and cares for me.

Leadership Secrets from Mary Magdalene

1. A leader knows God loves and cares for her personally.
2. A leader understands God empowers her and other women to be a voice for Him.
3. A leader realizes God continues to work in her life to change her for His glory.

Just for YOU

Be Still and Listen to What God Is Saying to You

- Mary Magdalene's responses to Jesus were based on her life-changing experiences with Him. As you think back on your experiences, how has God changed you? Today during your quiet moments with God, come with a heart of gratitude and focus on His blessings to you personally through both the good and bad times. Then be still and allow God to speak to you.

Write

- Describe how you have observed God working in your life. What is your story? How are you changing?

Do It Now

- As you consider the difficult times in your story, what one thing can you share about God's love for you with a friend who is going through her own dark night of the soul?

CHAPTER EIGHT

DARE TO DREAM: LYDIA
Acts 16

A rock pile ceases to be a rock pile
the moment a single man [or woman] contemplates it,
bearing within him [or her] the image of a cathedral.
Antoine de Saint-Exupery, French novelist

*L*ife after divorce is a very curious thing. It is simply life upside down. One Saturday I remember calling my daughter, Heather, who was away at college, and asking, "What should I do? I've been asked out on a date." After being married to the same man for more than a quarter of a century, the prospect of a date was overwhelming. I felt like a jittery teenager all over again.

"Don't worry, Mom," my daughter began. "Breathe. You'll do just fine. Just enjoy the time and have fun." As I hung up the phone, I asked myself, "What is wrong with this picture?" She was repeating to me advice I had given her only a couple of years earlier.

With my personal life in chaos and without the security of marriage and two-incomes, I experienced another crisis. Now my boss of sixteen years, Bill, decided he wanted to leave the world of consulting nonprofit organizations and go into the construction business. Building offices throughout the city where he resided had been his avocation for several years. As he approached the age of 50, he was ready for a major change in his life. He discussed closing the company, selling the company, dissolving the company. Whatever his choice, my position as a senior vice president was in jeopardy.

One evening in July 2001 as we met in Chicago to prepare for a meeting with a longtime client, I asked him to consider possibly allowing those of us who loved what we were doing to continue our relationships with the clients.

"Are you saying you want to start your own company with your clients?" he asked.

Well, no. That was not my intention. Can you imagine the risks that would involve? And me divorced, without a second stream of income. But I had started the conversation, so I continued . . . always being careful to tell the truth. "I have not figured out the 'how,'" I explained. "I simply wanted you to think about allowing some of us to continue working with the clients and people we love."

"So," he shot back, "what if I gave you the client relationships you have? Would you start your own company?" He was testing my courage and my nerve.

"Are you suggesting that you may give me my client relationships so I could start my own company?" I inquired not believing the words either of us were saying and not being at all comfortable with the risks I would be taking.

"Yes," he replied staring me in the eye.

In my true processing form, I told him, "If you are making me an offer, I will give you an answer in the morning." We shook, and the possibility of a deal was set. I would give him an answer in the morning.

I returned to my hotel room, stunned ... numb. I wasn't feeling. I was in that land just before you awaken when you are neither awake nor asleep. At the same time, my body felt like I had been slammed and run over by a tractor-trailer truck. Both the risks and possibilities were incredible. But there was no safety net. I immediately called my friend, Susan. I met Susan in the singles' Sunday school class I began attending shortly after my divorce. She became my prayer buddy, and we had shared our stories and our lives over several years.

"What do you think?" I asked her.

"I think God just answered your prayer," she replied. We spoke for several more minutes before I hung up the phone.

Of course, I spent the night in prayer, and I knew Susan was praying for me. But eventually God reminded me of a quote I had heard a female minister recite by Mark Twain, "Twenty years from now you will be more disappointed by the things you didn't do than by the ones you did." The next morning I told my boss I accepted his offer. I would go for it, and start my own company.

I launched R-Designs, Inc. in September 2001, and never looked back. Through the years, God blessed the company. He provided and allowed us to serve some incredible ministries and share our blessings with others. He brought people into my life just in time. God was encouraging me to dare to dream—"to become all I was capable of becoming." There was another woman who had a similar experience to mine. Her name was Lydia.

Meeting Lydia

Not on Paul's Agenda

Luke, the author of the book of Acts, introduces us to Lydia in Acts 16. Paul and his companions were on their second missionary journey headed for Asia when Paul had a vision. In his dream, Paul was visited by a man from Macedonia who begged, *"Come over to Macedonia and help us"* (Acts 16:9). Luke comments, *"After Paul had seen the vision, we got ready at once to leave for Macedonia concluding that God had called us to preach the gospel to them"* (Acts 16:10). The missionary troupe traveled through several cities and finally arrived in Philippi. Here the followers of Jesus met Lydia.

The Sabbath Meeting

Lydia was a successful businesswoman who dealt in purple cloth. Originally, she came from Thyatira, but at the time of our story, she was well established with her household in Philippi. Lydia worshipped God, and so on the Sabbath, she went outside the city wall to meet with a group of women in what was referred to as a place of prayer.

Luke explains that on a particular Sabbath when Paul and his companions were staying in Philippi, they went outside the city to the river looking for the place of prayer. When they located the meeting place, Paul sat down and began speaking to the women gathered there—including Lydia.

Lydia's Response to Paul's Message

While Lydia listened to Paul, God opened her heart to respond to Paul's message (16:14). Lydia and her entire household were baptized. She then invited Paul and his companions to stay in her home, or as Luke explains the situation, *"And she persuaded us"* (Acts 16:15).

A Final Meeting with Lydia

The last time scripture refers to Lydia is in Acts 16:40. Paul and Silas were released from prison and returned to Lydia's house of safety and comfort where they encouraged the new congregation of believers before they left to continue their missionary journey. The house church that met at Lydia's eventually grew into the Church of Philippi to whom Paul wrote Philippians.

Lydia as a Leader for God

From our brief encounter with Lydia, we learn that Lydia leads based on her strengths. She is a woman who was successful in business. She used her resources to support and serve Paul and his companions in their missionary endeavors. She provided a haven for the missionaries, which became the ministry center for her city. In many ways, we could consider her the founding mother of the Church at Philippi.

Many businesswomen, like Lydia, have the opportunity to use their resources to lead through giving. One businesswoman who supported numerous ministries during her lifetime was Mary Crowley. Crowley taught "God blesses us so we can bless others." Crowley gave her time, her finances, and her encouragement to thousands of individuals. Consider what gifts God has given you, and how you can use those gifts to bless and encourage ministries and people.

My Response to Lydia

Through Lydia's story, I gained a new perspective on the Apostle Paul and his view of women. I had grown up believing that Paul taught a woman's role is to be silent and submissive. In this chapter of Acts, I see Paul encouraging women in their faith.

First, we see that Paul was unafraid to associate and join with a group of women in worshipping God. In fact, Paul instructed his disciple, Timothy, in I Timothy 5:1-2 to treat men as brothers and women as sisters. Paul advocated for an inclusive theology that recognized both men and women in the church and our ministries. One of the books I have found most helpful in exploring further the topic of brothers and sisters in Christ is *Mixed Ministry: Working Together as Brothers and Sisters in an Oversexed Society* by Sue Edwards, Kelley Mathews, and Henry J. Rogers.[1] As we have seen earlier, God created us male and female. He made sexuality a part of our DNA as human beings. As the book mentioned above explains, we need transformation, not segregation.

Second, we see Paul instructing women in biblical truth. He sat down on the riverbank and taught the women God's Word.

Third, Paul recognized the work of the Holy Spirit in Lydia's life and baptized her and her household. Each of us needs to be personally responsible to listen actively to God's direction in our lives. As we observe in Acts 16:14, God opened Lydia's heart to respond when she listened to His Word. God wants to open your heart to His message so you will respond, but we must be in the practice of listening.

I also see in Lydia's story the simple fact that Lydia responds to God's message. But she does not stop there. She then encourages her household to respond. Scripture does not tell us how she got her household to respond, but positive encouragement, not nagging, is useful.

Leadership Secrets from Lydia

1. A leader recognizes that God created men and women to work together.
2. A leader understands her need to be taught scripture and then to teach others.
3. A leader recognizes her personal responsibility to respond to God's voice.
4. A leader realizes she is blessed so she can share and bless others.

Just For YOU

Be Still and Listen to What God Is Saying to You

- Spend time listening to how God wants to empower you to make a difference in the world for Him. What are the dreams He has placed in your heart?

Write

- Put your heartfelt dreams on paper—even if you have never revealed them to anyone before.
- Identify what is keeping you from your dreams. Ask God to help you conquer your fears.

Do It Now

- In the next twenty-four hours with God's help, take one step toward making your dreams become reality.

CHAPTER NINE

ONE WOMAN CAN MAKE THE DIFFERENCE: THE WISE WOMAN OF ABEL

2 Samuel 20:14-22

What passion would give you the courage to move mountains?
Joanna Barsh

*A*fter my marriage ended, if you had told me God was going to bless me beyond my wildest imagination and give me the true desires of my heart, I would have stared at you incredulously. But God's ways are not our ways. God has blessed me beyond anything I could ask, hope or think. I am continually reminded of God's words written through the prophet Jeremiah which appear in Jeremiah 29:11:

"I know the plans I have for you," declares the Lord,
"plans to prosper you and not to harm you,
plans to give you hope and a future."

I can see the truth today, but back then I was clueless. I had little faith in God at that moment. Everything I hoped for, longed for, and

92

worked for—from my limited vision—seemed gone. I could not hear or understand how God loved me. I saw God as more concerned about my obedience to the religious rules rather than interested in a relationship with me. My focus was on being less so I could avoid being prideful, rather than pushing myself to be my best as a reflection of my God. Through my personal crises, everything changed.

In Margaret Wheatley's book, *Leadership and the New Science*,[1] I discovered an instruction manual for how to navigate life during turbulent times. Wheatley writes about finding a "teacher" in the wilderness of Colorado while standing in the middle of a river. The river is seeking its path to the ocean while it constantly changes from a babbling brook, to white rapids, to a wide gentle river. The river possesses an internal faith it will arrive at the ocean, but it does so through the disorder and chaos of change.

I believe as the psalmist wrote in Psalm 16:11, that God will indeed show you and me the path of life. What I am realizing, however, is that the path is revealed to me in incremental steps. God's GPS only lets me see the next turn, not my final destination.

After my divorce, I secured my Master of Arts degree, turned 50 and joined AARP (American Association of Retired Persons). I remarried, expanded the family by one stepdaughter, a new son-in-law, and daughter-in-law, and began working toward my PhD. Life continues to be about new beginnings.

In my "life after 50," I searched scripture for new models of wisdom. I discovered Moses was 80 when God called him from the wilderness to lead the children of Israel (Ex 7:7). Somehow my biblical teaching had not only overlooked gender, but also age. There is no retirement in scripture. The concept of new beginnings is open to any of us—at whatever age.

God also opened the door for me to discover spiritual direction. I had worked with several professionals in order to help me heal the emotional pain in my life from a psychological perspective. I knew, however, I was damaged spiritually. I had a hole in my soul. I needed help healing spiritually, and so God provided me a spiritual director, a type of spiritual counselor, Janet Davis.[2]

"What is spiritual direction?" you ask. The concept is centuries old and built on the premise that God seeks a personal relationship, even a friendship with us as individuals, and that spiritual direction can help us meet our desire and God's for such a friendship.[3] Spiritual direction assists an individual in developing and cultivating a personal relationship with God. The practice recognizes that God speaks to individuals including you and me today. As Alan Jones writes: "The art of spiritual direction lies in our uncovering the obvious in our lives and in realizing that everyday events are the means by which God tries to reach us."[4] It is about helping us hear the voice of God in the everydayness of our lives.

During my spiritual growth process, Janet introduced me to a poem entitled, "The Jump" by Mary Anne Radmacher who graciously gave permission to use her poem. It reminded me how afraid I was of letting go to become the person God wanted me to be.

the

jump

is

so

frightening between

where

i

am and

94

where i want to be ...
because of
all i may become
i will
close my eyes
and leap![5]

What would I become, I wondered, if I put down my walls and became who I really am—the "me" God created? As I worked with this thought and continued to study God's Word, I came across a biblical woman whom I did not remember meeting. I liked her immediately because she was a woman whose actions demanded courage. Maybe she could help inspire me to be courageous.

Meeting the Woman of Abel

The woman of Abel didn't happen to live in Jesus' time like so many of the women we have met. She was not selected for a position of authority like Deborah. In fact, this woman is so "unknown" that the writers of scripture did not even remember her name. She is simply known as the wise woman of Abel, and you can find her in 2 Samuel 20. She is a woman whose passion gave her the courage to act in order to save the people in her city.

The Context

I must begin by confessing that before writing this book, I never had studied the book of 2 Samuel. The book is about the reign of King David after Saul dies. It is a book about David's wars, David's peace agreements, David's wives and his dysfunctional family. When David's kids were mad at their father, they killed each other or raped some of David's wives. Not exactly the type of book I would choose to read. Buried, however, in the pages of 2 Samuel is the story about the wise woman of Abel.

By the time we get to 2 Samuel 20, the army of David was in disarray. One of the troublemakers was a man named Sheba from the tribe of Benjamin, who rebelled against David and led his men away from Jerusalem. David was concerned about Sheba, so he sent his army after him led by Captain Joab. Sheba had gathered his men and together they took shelter in the town of Abel. Joab and his troops then surrounded Abel, made a dirt ramp up the city wall, and began battering the wall to knock it down. The stage is set.

The Story

Scripture explains that the wise woman of Abel did not understand why Joab and his men were attacking her city. Immediately the woman sprung into action as a leader motivated by passion for her city. She courageously stood on the top of the wall and began to yell: *"Listen! Listen! Tell Joab to come here so I can speak to him"* (20:16). The wise woman of Abel opened the doors of communication—and she went to the top—the top of the wall and the top of the chain of command.

Joab soon arrived at the city wall, and the woman requested, *"Listen to what your servant has to say"* (20:17). Joab responded affirmatively, *"I am listening."*

The woman began with a history lesson about her town of Abel that used to be the place where people throughout Israel went for good advice or to settle a problem (20:18). She then reminded Joab, *"We are the peaceful and faithful in Israel. You are trying to destroy a city that is a mother in Israel. Why do you want to swallow up the Lord's inheritance?"* (20:19).

Joab explained that he was not trying to destroy the people of Abel, but that there was a man who was the leader of a rebellion against King David hiding in the city. *"Hand over this one man,"* Joab commented, *"and I'll withdraw from the city"* (20:21).

The wise woman of Abel not only promised to give the rebel to Joab; she took a further step and stated, *"We will throw his head over the wall"* (20:21, CEV).

The woman left Joab and went to the townspeople. With her wisdom, she persuaded them to do as she promised. They cutoff Sheba's head and threw it over the wall to Joab (20:22). Joab then blew a signal on his trumpet. The soldiers left the walls of Abel to return to their own homes, and Joab went back to report to King David in Jerusalem (20:22).

The Wise Woman of Abel as a Leader for God

This woman is a revolutionary leader because her leadership results in radical change. She singlehandedly saved her city from destruction. As we examine this unnamed biblical woman through the lens of leadership, we can glean several truths about her leadership style.

First, from a human perspective, God does not seem to choose this woman. She chose herself. We have no record that God spoke to her. Clearly, she was a woman acting without authority or a position, but God validated her actions by preserving this woman's leadership story in the pages of scripture.

Second, this woman sees a need, and she chooses to take action. Her city was under attack. She did not talk. She did not gain permission from the city council or follow the chain of command. She simply went to the top in order to get the job done, and courageously asked to speak to Joab.

Third, this woman is knowledgeable about the history of her city related to Israel and God. When she spoke to Joab she reminded him of how the city provided a service to the leaders of Israel. She claimed the people of Abel were God's people.

Fourth, this woman takes responsibility for her city. When Joab explained that he did not want to destroy Abel, but he needed to capture Sheba, the woman promised that the city would act by throwing Sheba's head over the wall to Joab. She is a leader making deals for her city.

Finally, as a leader, the wise woman of Abel persuaded the townspeople to act as she had promised Joab. The woman models Phillips's definition of a leader by persuading the city's citizens to act for their shared goal of saving their city. Peace again returned to Abel.

My Response to the Woman of Abel

The woman of Abel reminds me of the difference one woman can make when she chooses to be a servant leader and act. This woman's passion was to save her town. In the town's moment of need, she acted as a true servant leader "caring, inspiring, and persuading others to act for certain shared goals."[6] The question you and I must each ask ourselves is: What is your passion? How does God want to use you and your story?

For me, I did finish my PhD. Then using some of my retirement dollars, I gave myself the space and time to write this book. My passion, based on my personal journey, is to share the freedom we, as women, have in Christ to lead.

As you consider where you are in your life, stop and consider how God may want to use you to make a difference in His world. The critical issue to consider is: What is your God-given passion?

Leadership Secrets from the Wise Woman of Abel

1. A leader recognizes God puts passion and desires in her heart. She is sensitive to the needs of certain people.
2. A leader trusts that God will give her the wisdom to know how to act to make a difference.
3. A leader understands that leadership requires courage, being willing to act at times without authority or permission.
4. A leader knows that leadership involves persuading others to take action with you.
5. A leader remembers that one woman with God can make the difference.

Just for YOU

Be Still and Listen to What God Is Saying to You
- What concerns are you truly passionate about? As you listen to God speak to you, do you believe He is also concerned about that issue or group of people?
- Ask God for the wisdom and courage about how He wants to empower you to make a difference based on your passion.

Write
- Write about why you are passionate about the specific issue(s). What has happened in your life to sensitize you to these concerns?
- Write down five things you could do to make a difference for what you are passionate about.

Do It Now
- Do one thing from your list above to begin making a difference for the people or issue for which you are passionate.

CHAPTER TEN

CHOOSING THE BEST: MARY OF BETHANY

Luke 10:38-42 and John 12:1-8

You are not a human being in search of a spiritual experience.
You are a spiritual being immersed in a human experience.
Pierre Teilhard de Chardin

I glanced at the kitchen calendar—July 20, 2009. The comprehensive exams for my PhD were only three short weeks away. Anything and everything that was covered during the sixty-hours of my doctoral academic career could be on the test. Some of the other members of my cohort had started studying in January. I studied some during the spring, but waited until the middle of May to zero-in on the task. I worked fulltime and needed to finish the final semester's work first. During the summer, we each were required to complete an internship. I can't speak for my cohort members, but I was exhausted.

As I perused the emails of my classmates, I sensed panic rising in many of us. For four years, my classmates and I studied together— reading, writing, and working harder than most of us imagined possible preparing for this dream of a doctoral degree. Now everything

100

hung in the balance. All I had studied for and worked for rested on this one exam. There would be one day of written exams: one question in the morning and one question in the afternoon. Each question was evaluated: pass or fail. The following day I was responsible to make an hour-long presentation on my twelve-hours of independent studies. If one failed to make the mark there would be only one more chance for redemption—sometime during the following January.

I still needed to complete the final two papers for my internship. How had the days slipped by so fast? The day was almost over. I remember checking the clock and noticing it was about 9:00 p.m. Then the phone rang.

"Mom, we have a healthy, baby boy," my son began. "But Lis (my son's term of endearment for his wife) is not doing so well."

My son and daughter-in-law were expecting their first child—their miracle baby after years of disappointment and loss—and a king's ransom in medical bills. As my son explained, during the birthing process things went terribly wrong.

For two hours, my daughter-in-law writhed in pain. When the medical personnel finally checked, Lisa was freezing cold. Her blood pressure had dropped to 60/40. She was bleeding to death. She was rushed back into surgery for two-and-a-half hours where the doctor discovered one of the main uterine arteries was not closed off. She was given seven units of blood. Now Lisa was in intensive care and my son carried the entire weight of his young family on his shoulders. I am not sure what empty words I mumbled, trying to reassure my son of my love and prayers. Words are so useless in times of crisis. Then the call ended.

And I sat alone in the silence of my empty house.

Did I hear it? Did I hear that unspoken cry for help in my son's voice? Suddenly nothing else mattered. I knew I had to go to the hospital and help Dave. David needed me. He needed support. I immediately called and told him I was coming in the morning to help him.

"Could you come now?" he asked.

"No." I responded as a realist. We live in Plano, Texas. Dave and Lisa live in The Woodlands outside of Houston—about a four-hour drive.

"I can't drive safely that far tonight," I told Dave. I am a morning person, and it was already now past 9 p.m. "I'll leave here around five, and see you before 9 a.m."

When I arrived at the hospital the next morning and gave my son a hug, I felt relief spread throughout his entire body. Finally someone was here to help carry his burden.

My son and I had met in the birthing center room, but there was no mother and no baby. Dave took me first to the neonatal intensive care unit (NICU) where his son stayed while Dave went up several floors to visit Lisa. He proudly showed me his newborn son. Tyce was definitely the biggest baby in the NICU that morning.

Then he took me up several floors to visit with Lisa. I remember seeing this new mother so weak and ghostly gray. She had not even had the opportunity to meet and hold her son. For the next 48 hours, she remained in the intensive care unit of the hospital.

Choices. As my son recounts, when my daughter-in-law's life was in jeopardy, I "dropped everything" and traveled to the hospital in The Woodlands, Texas, to support my son. I was given the awesome privilege to help care for baby Tyce and to stand with my son while he dealt with the weight of a newborn son and his wife up in ICU. I was there at the family's point of need, and helped my son not feel alone in caring for his young family.[1]

I was privileged to spend my first night in the birthing center with Dave and his son, Tyce. We got up to feed Tyce at 11 p.m., 3 a.m. and 6 a.m., and I thanked God that He gave new babies to mommies and daddies, not "nanas." I was in the room with Tyce when Lisa was finally brought back and introduced to her little boy. I was given an incredible gift to be part of my son's family and to bond with my son, daughter-in-law, and grandson in a new way. I understood something very special happened as I walked with my son's family, caring and sharing through life's difficult times.

Meeting Mary of Bethany

Choices—we all have them, and we all make them. There is a Bible story of two women who made different choices. The women are Martha and Mary, the two sisters of Lazarus whom we met earlier in chapter four. This particular story of their lives is told in Luke 10:38-42.

Jesus traveled with His disciples through a particular village where Martha made the choice to open her home to Him. The author, Luke, then tells the reader that Martha had a sister named Mary who chose to sit at the feet of Jesus and listen to His teachings. Meanwhile Martha was *"distracted by all the preparations that had to be made"* (10:40). She came to Jesus and asked, *"Lord, don't you care that my sister has left me to do the work by myself?"* (10: 40).

Jesus lovingly responded to Martha validating her feelings, *"Martha, Martha, … you are worried and upset about many things"* (10:41). Jesus then contrasted Martha's hurried, stressed internal state with something else when he said, *"but only one thing is needed"* (10:42). Jesus then celebrated Mary's "better" choice stating, *"and it will not be taken away from her"* (10:42).

Often when Bible teachers focus on this passage, they speak directly to the women in their audience and ask: Which of the women are you most like—a Martha or a Mary? I hope you understand that God does not want you to be like Martha or Mary; He simply wants you to be you yourself—authentically you. So what is Jesus saying?

What Is the "Good Part"?

Contextually, Jesus contrasted the internal state of Martha's soul with that of Mary's.[2] He told Martha that she was worried and troubled. Martha was trying to be the perfect hostess and with the pressure of getting the dinner on the table, she was irritable, grumpy, and stressed! In contrast, Mary chose something different—quiet and stillness. She was internally at peace feeding her soul at the feet of Jesus, focusing on the spiritual aspect of her life. Mary was making time for herself. As women, there are numerous things that compete for our time, but we can make choices. Perhaps, we can even choose like Mary the "good part." Consider these several situations.

- Your toddler has finally gone to sleep for her nap. Do you get busy folding clothes and straightening the house, or do you take time for yourself—choosing peace instead of busyness?
- You are hosting a women's Bible study and dessert at your home, and you are running out of time. Do you take two hours and make that incredible chocolate delight dessert from scratch, or go and buy "just-made" brownies from your neighborhood supermarket?
- You need to write a proposal today. You have this gnawing sensation that you first need to make time and take a walk for thirty minutes. Do you move to your desk to write the proposal, or do you listen to your inner voice and take the walk first?

God has not left us alone to make the choices of our lives, but in order to hear His voice, we must take time to be still and quiet. There are numerous verses that remind us to be quiet in order to know God and our own internal strengths.

"Be still, and know that I am God" (Ps 46:10).
"In quietness and trust is your strength" (Is 30:15).

Will you set aside time in your day to be still? As Dana Scully said to her partner in one episode of the *X-Files*, "I think God is speaking. I just don't think anyone is listening." Will you commit to making a time to position yourself to be quiet so you can listen to God? He wants to speak to you.

Another Glimpse of Mary

I want to return to John 11 and the story of Lazarus, not to rehash the story, but to remind us of the differences between these two women and their response to Jesus. Both sisters met Jesus with the same comment: *"Lord, if you had been here, my brother would not have died"* (John 11:21, 32). Martha, in meeting Jesus continued talking. She was a woman who responded intellectually with her head. Mary, on the other hand, came to Jesus and fell down at His feet weeping. She responded emotionally from her heart. The story demonstrates again the truth that Jesus responds to each of us as individuals—just as we are. He does not ask you to be a Martha or a Mary. He simply asks you to be you—His precious daughter.

A Final Look at Mary of Bethany

In John 12:1-8, we get a final look at Mary. Jesus was once again in the home of the three siblings: Martha, Lazarus and Mary, and each was responding in his or her own way. Scripture records that *"they made Him a supper"* (12:2, KJV), so perhaps all of them helped make the dinner this time. Martha was serving; Lazarus was sitting at the table with Jesus; Mary came to Jesus with some very expensive perfume, which she opened and then anointed the feet of Jesus. She demonstrated her love and devotion to her Savior with a gift.

The anointing caused some stir among the disciples, and Judas Iscariot asked, *"Why wasn't this perfume sold and the money given to the poor? It was worth a year's wages"* (John 12:5). The author of the gospel explains that Judas made the comment not because he was kindhearted and concerned about the poor, but because he was a thief.

Jesus responded to Judas by stating, *"Leave her alone, ... It was intended, that she should save this perfume for the day of my burial. You will always have the poor among you, but you will not always have me"* (John 12:7-8). Like her sister, Mary knew firsthand the experience of death and loss. Could she therefore possibly have understood that Jesus was telling His disciples that He was going to die shortly? At this dinner party where the Bethany siblings were hosting Jesus and the disciples, Mary celebrated Jesus in her own way—as a person, as her God.

So often as I care for the people whom I love including my family, I can get wrapped up in the busyness of doing for them and forget to be simply with them. Mary was here with Jesus—honoring who He was in deed and with her presence.

Mary as a Leader for God

Because scripture gives us only these several brief glances of Mary of Bethany, I am curious to know more about this particular woman. Who is she? How did she meet Jesus? What is her story? I want to meet her. What I do see in the biblical accounts about Mary is a woman who as a leader reflects the "Free-to-Lead" leadership model.

First, Mary led authentically. She knew who she was and chose to act from her inner core even when others criticized her. In the passages we examined, we observed Mary being criticized by Martha and Judas. Their comments did not cause her to change her actions. At Lazarus's burial, Mary was comfortable in her tears and grieving. She was vulnerable and honest with whom she authentically was.

Second, Mary led based on her personal strengths. Scripture reveals Mary as an intelligent, sensitive, generous individual. Although Mary could have been in the kitchen serving with her sister, Martha, Mary chose to focus on her gifts, not simply her skills.

As women, we sometimes confuse our strengths and our skills. When we use our strengths, we feel empowered, energized, and invigorated. When we use our skills, we may feel satisfied when a job is complete, but our inner soul has not been fed.

For example, I am strong both in writing and math, but writing is my strength, my love. Math is a skill I acquired. When I write something I choose, I have an inner energy and enthusiasm as I approach the project even if it is difficult and challenging. When I work on a math project, I approach the project as a job or a chore, not a love. There is no soul connection. Mary led from her strengths—her gifts.

Finally, Mary led with a servant heart. In anointing Jesus, she served her Lord in a loving and caring way. As a leader, she is taking action and ministering to the Son of God only a few days before His death. Mary gave her best to her Lord as an expression of gratitude, love and worship. Mary's action also demonstrates a gift she had. She was a woman with resources. Using our material gifts strategically, intelligently, and purposefully, allows us to lead through giving as servant leaders.

My Response to Mary

Three things stand out to me as I look at the life of Mary—three things I would like to replicate in my life and leadership. First I see Mary as a woman who practices caring for herself. She focuses on what is important to her, rather than merely living up to someone else's standards or expectations. Mary does not get caught up in the busyness of others. She does not become distracted by meeting the needs of others. She knows who she is. She knows what she wants. I appreciate the description by Elisa Morgan, President Emerita of MOPS International, of women who are always meeting everyone else's needs. She calls them "empty juice boxes with fifteen straws." I've been there. I've done that. I want to practice self-care, which includes focusing on who I am and what my unique gifts are.

Second, I glimpse Mary as a woman with the courage to express her voice, her heart. Mary's anointing the feet of Jesus was not a hidden expression of love and worship. She was courageously demonstrating her love and appreciation for the Savior. The disciples were present. Her family was there. And Mary chose to embrace her inner gratitude for Jesus by anointing His feet with a very expensive bottle of perfume and then wiping His feet with her hair. The disciples not only observed her act of devotion, but her action permeated the entire house filling it with the fragrance of the ointment. How often I struggle with finding the courage to take certain actions or express my true feelings or my authentic story.

Third, I observe Mary as someone who chooses to give her best. At times, my religious tradition instructed me to focus on practicing humility and being "last—not first," so I sometimes hid my true talents or gifts particularly when working in religious circles. Mary gave Jesus her best. To give my best, I must be willing to work hard, take risks, step out on a limb, and give up my false sense of security. Maybe you too have hidden some of your talents. Imagine what you could become if you focused your energies on what you can do and continued to work toward being your best. How could God empower you to advance His kingdom?

Leadership Secrets from Mary of Bethany

1. A leader understands God can respond to her when she is honestly and authentically herself.
2. A leader knows God wants to communicate to and through her, so she sets aside time to be quiet so she can hear His voice.
3. A leader is aware of her God-given gifts and focuses on using them.
4. A leader focuses on being her best as she serves God, which includes practicing self-care.
5. A leader practices being courageous as she listens and responds to God's direction.

Just for YOU

Be Still and Listen to What God Is Saying to You

- How do you create a special time and/or place where you can be still with God?
- Changing the place where you are still with God can sometimes help you see and hear God differently. Maybe you would like to take a walk outside in nature. Maybe you want to sit in the chapel of a local church or even an art museum—someplace where the sunlight pours through a window of colored glass. Where can you best hear God speak to you?

Write

- What did God say to you when you spent time alone with Him? Give expression to your thoughts and feelings in whatever manner you choose.
- Mary practiced self-care, following her heart. How are you taking care of yourself—the precious, child of God? How would you like to take care of yourself in the future?

Do It Now

- What one thing can you do to take care of yourself today? Do it!

NEXT STEPS

I am always doing things I can't do; that's how I get to do them.
Pablo Picasso

Thank you for joining me on this journey as together we examined the lives of these ten women from the pages of scripture through the lens of leadership. I hope you began answering for yourself the question: What does the Bible teach about women and leadership?

My desire is that you will apply the lessons you learned to your life and leadership. Like Esther, you will discover your voice. Like Rahab, you will act with courage. Like Deborah, you will lead with kindness. Like Martha, you will share the message God gave you. Like Mary—the mother of Jesus, you will be sensitive to the needs of those around you. Like the woman of Samaria, you will seek others who need to hear God's message. Like Mary Magdalene, you will sense God's love for you during your challenging times. Like Lydia, you will open your heart to God's message. Like the woman of Abel, you will follow your passions and make a difference in your world. Like Mary of Bethany, you will step away from busyness in order to care for yourself and give God your best.

I pray that God will bless you abundantly as you explore your freedom to lead.

ACKNOWLEDGMENTS

$\mathcal{J}$ am grateful for the many individuals who invested in me. Without them, I would not have found the courage to believe "I can." I want to begin by thanking my three bosses who opened doors and gave me opportunities to succeed professionally: Dr. John Walvoord, Jim Killion, and Bill Jester. They believed in me before I believed in myself.

I appreciate so much the faculty members at Dallas Baptist University who pushed me intellectually as I studied leadership and then focused my research on women and leadership. In particular, I want to recognize Dr. Sue Kavli, Dr. Stephen Stookey, Dr. Gail Wallace, and Dr. Michael Williams, Sr. I am also indebted to Ruth Shanahan, Andy Horner, Bonnie Kelley, and Reba Jeter for their information on the life and leadership of Mary C. Crowley—the woman who became my personal leadership mentor through her writings and stories.

For my writing support and encouragement, I want to thank Linda Friesen who read the first draft of my book and gave me helpful guidance and feedback from a biblical perspective. I am also grateful for my editor Amy Baggett who diligently read each word of this book numerous times always offering her expertise and wisdom in a positive, but honest way. She helped me find logic and structure as

I meandered through the lives of the ten biblical women. I am also grateful for the numerous women God has put in my life to model for me what a Christian female leader looks like: Janet Davis, Elisa Morgan, Carolyn Custis James, and Jan Winebrenner. Thank you for leading the way.

For my two children, Dave and Heather, who walked life's journey with me, thank you for your support. You are my teachers, and I am so grateful for your love and your lives. I am always learning from you both. Finally, I want to express my deepest gratitude to my husband, Kris. Without you, your support, and your encouragement, this book would only be a dream and not a reality. Thank you for granting me the space in our lives, our income, and our home to complete this project. I love you always.

NOTES
✤

Introduction

[1] Ronald A. Heifetz, *Leadership without Easy Answers* (London: The Belknap Press, 1994), 184.

[2] For a broader discussion on the topic of women and leadership, see Alan F. Johnson, ed., *How I Changed my Mind about Women in Leadership: Compelling Stories from Prominent Evangelicals* (Grand Rapids, MI: Zondervan, 2010).

[3] James M. Kouzes and Barry Z. Posner, *The Leadership Challenge*, 3rd ed. (San Francisco: Jossey-Bass, 2002), xxiii.

[4] Donald T. Phillips bases his leadership definition on the work of James MacGregor Burns, *Martin Luther King, Jr. On Leadership: Inspiration & Wisdom for Challenging Times* (New York: Warner Business, 1998), 23.

[5] Ibid.

[6] This leadership model is based on my analysis of the leadership of Mary Crowley and identified in my dissertation, Rita M. Carver, "The Leadership of Mary C. Crowley: Pioneer Female Business Leader" (PhD diss., Dallas Baptist University, 2011).

Mary C. Crowley

[1] Mary C. Crowley, *You Can Too* (Old Tappan, NJ: Fleming H. Revell Co., 1980), 60.

[2] Holly G. Miller, "The First Lady of Home Interiors," *The Saturday Evening Post*, repr., April 1983. The total numbers of displayers and gross annual sales fluctuated each year.

[3] Richard C. Bartlett, *The Direct Option* (College Station, TX: Texas A&M University Press, 1994), 170.

[4] Rita M. Carver, "The Leadership of Mary C. Crowley: Pioneer Female Business Leader" (PhD diss., Dallas Baptist University, 2011).

Chapter One—Without a Voice: Esther

[1] Paul Laurence Dunbar, *The Complete Poems of Paul Laurence Dunbar* (New York: Dodd, Mead & Company, 1913), 71, Project Gutenberg EBook, http://archive.org/details/thecompletepoems18338gut (accessed April 22, 2013). The poem was first published in 1896 and exists in the public domain.

[2] C. F. Keil, *Commentary on the Old Testament in Ten Volumes,* vol. III, ed. C. F. Keil and F. Delitzsch, trans. by Sophia Taylor (Grand Rapids, MI: William B. Eerdmans Publishing Company, 1973), 337.

[3] Harold Myra and Marshall Shelley, *The Leadership Secrets of Billy Graham* (Grand Rapids, MI: Zondervan, 2005), 19.

[4] Donald T. Phillips, *Martin Luther King, Jr. on Leadership: Inspiration & Wisdom for Challenging Times* (New York: Warner Business, 1998), 23.

Chapter Two—A Woman with a Plan: Rahab

[1] C. F. Keil and F. Delitzsch, *Commentary on the Old Testament in Ten Volumes,* vol. II, trans. by James Martin (Grand Rapids, MI: William B. Eerdmans Publishing Company, 1973), 33.

[2] David M. Howard, Jr., *Joshua* in *The New American Commentary,* vol. 5, ed. E. Ray Clendenen (Nashville, TN: Broadman and Holman Publishers, 1998), 107-108.

Chapter Three—Sometimes a Warrior: Deborah

[1] Mary C. Crowley, *String of Pearls: Secrets of Wisdom and Fulfillment* (Waco, TX: Word Books, 1985), 45.

[2] K. Lawson Younger, Jr., *Judges and Ruth: The NIV Application Commentary from Biblical Text ... to Contemporary Life* (Grand Rapids, MI: Zondervan, 2002), 140.

[3] Ibid., 21.

[4] James M. Kouzes and Barry Z. Posner, *The Leadership Challenge,* 3rd ed. (San Francisco, CA: Jossey-Bass, 2002), xxiv.

Chapter Four—The Shadow of Death: Martha

[1] To finish my personal story, God continued to watch over my brother's wife and their two children. Several years after Bob's death, his wife remarried. God blessed her and her husband with several more children. Today the family lives in Missouri.

Chapter Five—Peace Beyond Understanding: Mary, the Mother of Jesus

[1] Merrill C. Tenney, *The Expositor's Bible Commentary with the New International Version of the Holy Bible,* vol. 9, *(John-Acts)* ed.

Frank E. Gaebelein. (Grand Rapids, MI: Zondervan Publishing House, 1981), 42.

[2] Francis J. Moloney, *The Gospel of John,* vol. 4 in *Sacra Paging Series,* ed. Daniel J. Harrington (Collegeville, MN: The Liturgical Press, 1998), 68.

[3] Gerald L. Borchert, *John 1-11* vol. 25A in *The New American Commentary: An Exegetical and Theological Exposition of Holy Scripture,* ed. E. Ray Clendenen (Nashville, TN: Broadman & Holman Publishers, 1996), 155.

Chapter Six—Damaged Goods: The Woman of Samaria

[1] Anne Graham Lotz, *Just Give Me Jesus* (Nashville, TN: W. Publishing Group, 2000), 95.

[2] Gerald L. Borchert, *John 1-11* vol. 25A in *The New American Commentary: An Exegetical and Theological Exposition of Holy Scripture,* ed. E. Ray Clendenen (Nashville, TN: Broadman & Holman Publishers, 1996), 210.

[3] James M. Kouzes and Barry Z. Posner, *The Leadership Challenge,* 3rd ed. (San Francisco: Jossey-Bass, 2002), xxiii.

[4] Brené Brown, *The Gifts of Imperfection: Let Go of Who You Think You're Supposed to Be and Embrace Who You Are* (Center City, MN: Hazelden, 2010), 50.

Chapter Seven—The Dark Night of the Soul: Mary Magdalene

[1] Janet Davis, *The Feminine Soul* (Colorado Springs, CO: NavPress, 2006), 12.

[2] Michael Gurian with Barbara Annis, *Leadership and the Sexes: Using Gender Science to Create Success in Business* (San Francisco: Jossey-Bass, 2008), 8.

[3] William Bridges, *Managing Transitions: Making the Most of Change* (Reading, MA: Addison-Wesley Publishing Co., 1991), 99-100.

Chapter Eight—Dare to Dream: Lydia

[1] Sue Edwards, Kelley Mathews, and Henry J. Rogers, *Mixed Ministry: Working Together as Brothers and Sister in an Oversexed Society* (Grand Rapids, MI: Kregel Publications, 2008).

Chapter Nine—One Woman Can Make the Difference: The Wise Woman of Abel

[1] Margaret J. Wheatley, *Leadership and the New Science: Discovering Order in a Chaotic World*, 3rd ed. (San Francisco: Berrett-Koehler Publishers, Inc., 2006).

[2] Janet Davis is a spiritual director, writer and speaker. She is the author of several books including *The Feminine Soul: Surprising Ways the Bible Speaks to Women* and *My Own Worst Enemy: How to Stop Holding Yourself Back*. You can learn more about her at www.janetdavisonline.com.

[3] William A. Barry and William J. Connolly, *The Practice of Spiritual Direction* (New York: HarperOne, 2009), xiii.

[4] Margaret Guenther, *Holy Listening: The Art of Spiritual Direction* (Lanham, MD: A Cowley Publications Book, 1992), ix.

[5] Mary Anne Radmacher, "The Jump," http://thinkexist.com/quotes/mary_anne_racmacher/ (accessed May 15, 2013). Used by permission of Mary Anne Radmacher. http://www.maryanneradmacher.net.

[6] Donald T. Phillips, *Martin Luther King, Jr. on Leadership: Inspiration & Wisdom for Challenging Times* (New York: Warner Business, 1998), 23.

Chapter Ten—Choosing the Best: Mary of Bethany

[1] Two years later when Dave and Lisa were expecting twins, it was Lisa's mother, Barbara Zimmer, who arrived to help our children. And yes, I took my comprehensive exams for my PhD on time, and passed them on my first attempt.

[2] J. W. Shephard, *The Christ of the Gospels: An Exegetical Study* (Grand Rapids, MI: Wm. B. Eerdmans Publishing Co., 1975), 375.

ABOUT THE AUTHOR

Dr. Rita White Carver is a leadership consultant, writer and educator who leads others to maximize their God-given potential. For more than thirty years, she perfected her skill of listening with the heart as well as the mind. Whether helping ministries define their vision or meeting with individuals to capture their passions, she digs beyond the surface to discover their deeper callings to help them become all they can be to make a difference for God in our world.

Rita works with nonprofit organizations in strategic planning, vision casting, and donor development. She also teaches at the University of Phoenix. Since completing her PhD at Dallas Baptist University in leadership studies, she is passionate about helping women discover the freedom they have to lead and become their best through leadership development.

Rita lives with her husband, Kris, in Plano, Texas. Together they have three grown children and five grandchildren. She enjoys nature, yoga, swimming, and learning. You can contact her at www.ritawhitecarver.com.

CPSIA information can be obtained at www.ICGtesting.com
Printed in the USA
LVOW06s0535020714

392573LV00002B/162/P